HOUSING
NEW ALTERNATIVES, NEW SYSTEMS

Manuel Gausa

Birkhäuser Publishers
Basel • Boston • Berlin

ACTAR Barcelona

This book looks assiduously at a number of recent residential schemes. Some of these were previously published in the review *Quaderns*, particularly in numbers 210 and 211, now out of print, the theoretical sections of which were devoted to the theme of housing, viewed as an "issue" that needs rethinking. The interest of the projects presented there, and now revised, along with subsequently compiled new material, most of it previously unpublished, has impelled this publication, focused on those emerging approaches which today define, with new vigor, contemporary residential planning.

The volume consists of two separate parts.
With a more theoretical bent, the first part glosses the lines of argument that underpin much current work of investigation, selection and structuration, centering on the exploration of those 'project dynamics' capable of generating new formal systems related to the phenomena of change which the contemporary city is currently undergoing.
The second part presents, by recourse to four independent thematic groups, a number of projects and built works judged to be paradigmatic of the new contemporary residential approach.
Both projects and built works thus combine to demonstrate some of the technical, spatial and formal possibilities inherent in the theoretical ideas expounded; ideas aimed in the last instance at an understanding of inhabited space as a potential interface, an intersection of forces somewhere between the general and the particular, the intimate and the collective.

I HOUSING: NEW ALTERNATIVES

- **9** 1. Dynamic Devices
- **15** 2. Commercial, Universal, Trivial
- **21** 3. Interior Landscape: 'Inhabited Units' and the residential cell
- **23** 3.1. Diversity rather than repetition
- **29** 3.2. Emptied-out rather than partitioned-off
- **31** 3.3. Flexibility rather than specialization
- **33** 3.4. Industrialization rather than handicraft
- **37** 3.5. New challenges: solutions in emergency situations- projects for the renovation of obsolete structures

II HOUSING: NEW URBAN IDEAS

- **41** 1. Housing-City-Territory
- **49** 2. Open Systems: Potential Encoders

  Structural Networks-Net-Dynamic Guidelines
- **53** A.1. Sequences: series, cadences, counterpoints
- **59** A.2. Webs: nets, rails, circuits

  Mixed Developments-Growth-Complex Formations
- **69** B.1. Outbreaks: profiles, excrescenses, inflexions
- **77** B.2. Maculae: grafts, parasitisms, commensalisms

  Open Spaces-Landscape-Manipulated Voids
- **83** C.1. Enclaves: fields, hollows, mattings
- **91** C.2. Terrains: contours, trenches, grounds

  Consolidated Fabrics-Dilation-Incisions/Excisions
- **99** Incisions/excisions: joints, breaches, abuttals
- **104** The project and the site: reactive mechanisms

OPEN SYSTEMS

- **112 Adriaan Geuze, West 8**
  Urban Plan. Borneo Sporenburg, Amsterdam
- **118 Ben van Berkel**
  Housing. Borneo Sporenburg, Amsterdam
- **122 MVRDV**
  Urban plan. Hoornse Kwadrant, Delft
- **126 Willem Jan Neutelings**
  Housing. Hollainhof, Ghent
- **130 Eduard Bru / Enric Serra, Lluís Vives, Jordi Cartagena**
  Urban plan. Poblenou seafront, Barcelona
- **134 Actar Arquitectura**
  Mixed residential mechanism, Graz
- **140 Dallas, Diacomidis, Haritos, Nikodimos, Papandreou**
  Urban Plan. Meyrin
- **144 Federico Soriano, Dolores Palacios**
  Urban Plan. Bilbao

BASIC UNITS / COMPLEX UNITS

- **152 Florian Riegler, Roger Riewe**
  Housing block. Graz
- **158 Kees Christiaanse**
  Housing block. Amersfoort
- **162 Willem Jan Neutelings**
  Semi-detached houses. Tilburg
- **168 Kas Oosterhuis**
  Dike housing. Groningen
- **172 Willem Jan Neutelings**
  Kustzone 4e Kwadrant. Huizen
- **178 Josep Lluís Mateo**
  Housing complex. Terrassa
- **182 Hans Kollhoff**
  Residential building. Amsterdam
- **188 Wiel Arets**
  Apartment tower. Amsterdam
- **192 Philippe Gazeau**
  Housing block. Paris
- **196 Francis Soler**
  Apartment building. Paris

HYBRID ENTITIES

- **204 Steven Holl**
  Makuhari housing. Chiba
- **210 Kas Oosterhuis**
  Dancing facades. Groningen
- **214 Willem Jan Neutelings**
  Prinsenhoek. Sittard
- **220 MVRDV**
  100 Wozoco's. Amsterdam

INCISIONS

- **234 Josep Llinàs**
  Dwellings in Ciutat Vella. Barcelona
- **240 Philippe Gazeau**
  Dwellings in the 19th Arrondissement. Paris
- **246 Francis Soler**
  Housing block. Paris
- **250 François Marzelle, Isabelle Manescau, Edouard Steeg**
  Apartments for immigrants. Bordeaux
- **254 Jean Nouvel**
  Housing and offices. Tours
- **258 Eduardo Souto de Moura**
  Housing block. Porto
- **264 Keim & Sill**
  Prefabricated housing and work units. Rathenow
- **272** Colophon

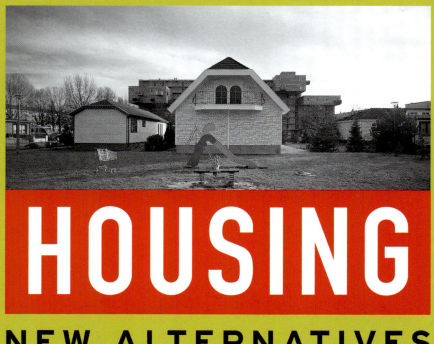

HOUSING
NEW ALTERNATIVES

]]]]]]]]]]

]

Wozoco building, Amsterdam.
(Architects: MVRDV, 1994-97)
Photo: Jordi Bernadó

1

DYNAMIC DEVICES

The different approaches to the theme of housing I've taken in recent years[1] are in fact framed by a more general personal preoccupation with exploring the particular limits of contemporary planning and its capacity for generating new formal contrivances that go beyond disciplinary habit or accepted convention (be it technical, typological or syntactical).
Devices relying on an optimistic 'formal invention' based on the construction of autonomous, intimate, subjective and unwonted plastic worlds, and on the definition of conceptual schemas that are more abstract and in direct relation to the interpretation of contemporary physical and cultural space.
A form understood–as **FERNANDO PORRAS** rightly suggests[2]–as a 'set of relationships capable of referring to possible diagrams which are tactical in reference, strategic tools intended to favor a more open correspondence between form and concept, reality and abstraction, this being understood in its most generative, evolutive and productive sense.'
A form which would appear, then, less as the meticulous outcome of a composition complete in itself than as but one combination among many; a 'paralyzed moment' in a **PROCESS** that, while interrupted, is theoretically open in time.

A FORM, IN SHORT, CONCEIVED MORE AS SYSTEM THAN AS COMPOSITION: OPEN SYSTEMS AS AGAINST CLOSED COMPOSITIONS.

Systems which would reveal their fitness to assume two important purposes:
▶ On the one hand, the definitive transference of the contemporary project from simple classical artifice–the more or less bizarre and ingenious deformation of the 'natural'–to the decidedly **ARTIFICIAL**–the autonomous, the unwonted, the 'new'.
▶ On the other, the specific capacity of contemporary culture for transcending the episodic and for directing action towards a structural process on a greater scale and in syntony with a new awareness of the specific landscape–physical and intellectual–generated around it.

---

1. The present text is a compilation of certain reflections already sketched out by the author in various articles (cf. 'Planes débiles o estrategias fuertes', *H/C* (catalogue), COAC, Barcelona, 1988; 'Systèmes ouverts vs. compositions fermées', *Europan III* (catalogue), Europan, Paris, 1994; 'Territorio y Mutabilidad,' in *You Are Here*, MACBA, Barcelona, 1995; 'Vivienda: nuevos sistemas urbanos,' in *Quaderns* 211, 1995; and 'De la metrópolis a la metápolis,' in *Quaderns* 213, 1996) and papers given in the seminars on this theme organized by Europan in Gävle and Rotterdam (1994) and Paris, Zagreb, Bucharest and Lisbon (1995-97). The author expresses his thanks to Didier Rebois, Mireille Appel Muller and Iorgis Simeoforidis for their help and their stimulating comments.
2. Cf. PORRAS, Fernando: Editorial in the journal *BAU 014*, 1996.

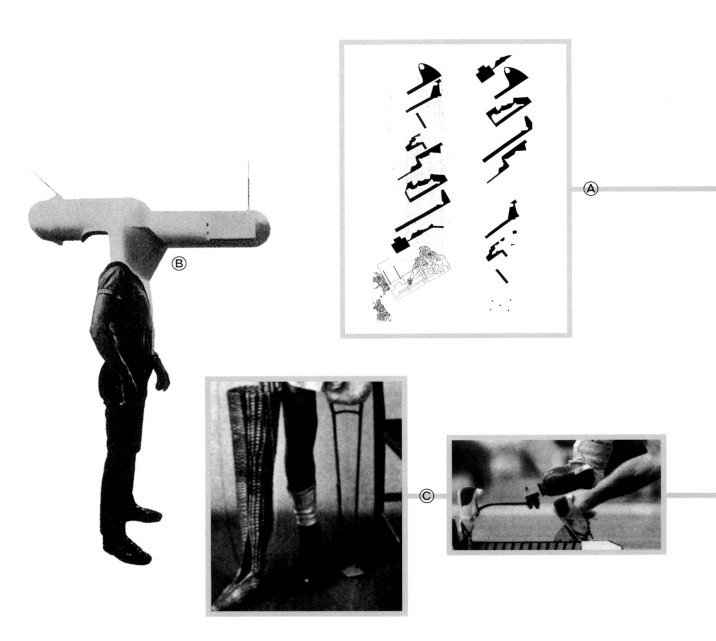

OF PARTICULAR INTEREST HERE, IN THAT SENSE, WOULD BE THOSE PROJECTURAL DEVICES CAPABLE OF FAVORING DYNAMIC PROCESSES AND–IN THE LAST ANALYSIS–SUDDEN 'CHANGES OF SCALE' IN THE SITE; changes of scale in which attention to the particular combines with those other, more general, references connected with the specific dynamics of transformation which the contemporary metropolis experiences today: 'changes of scale' associated with projects thought of as virtual epitomes of the city. PRECISE SYNTHESES, IN SHORT, OF THE VERY MOMENTS THAT DEFINE THE NEW URBAN SPACE OF TODAY.

The rigidity, predictability and permanence typical of the 'classical' city –and of the projectural parameters associated with it (control, figuration, stability)–have given way, in fact, to the indeterminacy and mutability of the contemporary city, which is otherwise more receptive to open structures with a capacity for evolution and perturbation. The substitution, in contemporary planning, of the closed idea of composition (the exact and designed appointing of the parts) for that of 'system' (an 'open' mechanism or vector ideogram capable of favoring varied combinations and different formal manifestations) thereby constitutes one of the prime examples of the change of paradigm which today characterizes the discipline.

Within this framework, the new 'prosthetic' vocation of contemporary architecture–described so tellingly by **MARC WIGLEY** in his many treatments of the subject[3]–does not reside so much in that ongoing situation of 'addiction' to an earlier corpus inherent in the architectural act itself as in the fact that–in distinction to classical thought, where any supplementation would still be realized in the image and likeness of an apparent, stable and immutable reality–this can no longer be the unique source of inspiration. ARCHITECTURE CANNOT NOW LIMIT ITSELF TO 'EXTENDING' THE CORPUS, BUT MUST BE AN ACTIVE AND FUNCTIONAL SUPPLEMENT TO IT, A MECHANISM THAT IS AUTONOMOUS AND RECEPTIVE TO A TIME BOTH 'ESTRANGED' AND SENSITIVE TO THE PARTICULAR, AND ALSO CAPABLE OF BEING SELF-GUIDING, OF SIMULTANEOUSLY PRIVILEGING THE HOST.

The media constantly confront us–in that sense the broadcasting of the Paralympic Games would prove particularly revelatory–with new mechanical artefacts that have nothing in common with the old handicapped limbs they supplant. They are functional and interchangeable elements; that is to say, mainly infrastructural, but in a time–and despite their assumed artifical aspect–whose situation of complicity with the receptive body is precise and incontrovertible, the better to optimize and transform its performance qualities.[4]

The authentic cultural dimension of contemporary architecture stems, in effect, from its disposition towards effectively confronting the apparent indefiniteness and debility of the reality that surrounds us, proceeding from a new logic that is more strategic than figurative, and which would no longer see the site (and the intersection of forces which criss-cross it) as an enveloping protector, a secure referent, but as an incomplete situation ripe for 'restructuring' and 'relaunching'.

IT IS THESE CONSIDERATIONS THAT INTEREST US TO EXPLORE VARIOUS NEW DYNAMICS ASSOCIATED WITH THE SUBJECT OF HOUSING: NOT ONLY FOR THE POTENTIAL RESPONSE THEY CONTAIN BUT FOR THE VOLITION IMPLICIT IN THEM TO SUGGEST NEW STRUCTURED PROCESSES WHEN CONFRONTED WITH THE CONSTANT SITUATION OF 'TENSION' AND 'LIMIT' WHICH CHARACTERIZES RESIDENTIAL SPACE.

A geographical limit and tension (belonging to those spaces which define the majority of actualized interventions), but also a disciplinary tension and limit (belonging to certain worn-out models, still based on now completely anachronistic semantic and technical parameters).

Ⓐ OMA. Urban ideograms for NSIA airport city (Seoul, 1995)

Ⓑ Hybrid gaze, polyhedral gaze, strategic gaze (In *SD* 4/95)

Ⓒ Classic prosthesis (evocative), modern (mechanical), contemporaneous (infrastructural)

Ⓓ Paradoxical territory: expectant landscape, real-estate landscape, potential landscape, real landscape (Mollet 1994. Photo: Jordi Bernadó)

---

3. Cf. WIGLEY, Marc: 'Prosthetic Theory: The Disciplining of Architecture,' in *Assemblage* 15, 1992, and *Ottagono* 96, 1992. **4.** Cf. GAUSA, Manuel & SALAZAR, Jaime: 'Retráctiles,' in *Quaderns* 199, 1993.

In effect, residential space demonstrates in a paradigmatic way the ongoing 'paradoxical state' of the contemporary territory: an articulated territory proceeding from the presence and epic potential of those structural operations of mobility and communication that are its backbone (capable of conjoining places and singular, unique, unusual events), yet which also evolve by figuratively reproducing (in those property deals which finally determine its identity) the prejudicial vulgarity of various strait-laced and inadequate models, both in the savings, spaces, uses and atmospheres they favor and in the iconographies and building techniques associated with them. *Prima materia* of the city, the theme of housing, thus comes up against the sclerotic paralysis of its own formulae, precisely because of the obligatory tribute the latter still pay to the tried and tested 'methods' of those already-built urbanist models advocated by the official discipline during the last twenty years: models trusting in a city 'imposed' anomalously on the territory. Little pipe dreams of order, harmony and homogeneity, suddenly bemused by the accelerated and unforeseen situation of coexistence that arises today with new, untamed areas of hybridization, contradiction and freedom specific not only to the current cultural and social fabric, but to the urban fabric itself: a fabric that is no longer unitary and complete but is instead the product of dynamic constants of transformation, combination, fracture and mutation.

A complex space, in short, which needs an operative, instrumental open space in order to generate 'catalysts of energy' rather than indifferent figures on an absent ground: 'operative landscapes' disposed on 'landscapes of intersection'; new relational geographies.

The trajectory proposed here attempts to illustrate the above considerations. Its objective is to try and ascertain the conceptual basis which inspires some of the new approaches tried, many of them parallel, simultaneous and surprisingly coincidental despite, curiously, having been frequently developed in widely differing fields.

ⓔ A patchwork of ideograms
1. MVRDV. WOZOCO building (Amsterdam, 1997)
2. Kazuyo Sejima. Low-level typology (Tokyo, 1995)
3. Willem Jan Neutelings. Hollainhof (Ghent, 1995-97)
4. MVRDV. Delft (1996)

SYSTEMS CHARACTERIZED BY MULTIFARIOUS STIMULAE AND INNER IMPULSES, AND GROUPED HERE—ACCORDING TO THE INTENSITY OF THE MOVEMENTS WHICH DEFINE THEM—IN OFTEN INTERSECTING AND OVERLAPPING CATEGORIES UNDERSTOOD MORE AS PLANNING DYNAMICS—STRUCTURAL MECHANISMS—THAN STRICT METHODOLOGICAL CLASSIFICATIONS;

categories which would seek to acknowledge a new and particularly complex projectural reality by retracing it, but also by marking it with other signs, other definitions, other analogies; that is, by other ways of looking that are more polyhedric than erudite, beginning with the conviction that to give new names to things, to propose unexpected associations or to discover other relationships, permits, as of now, new maps to be created[5]. Keys more than labels, then, whose purpose is to outline, starting from three kinds of approach, some of the more significant aspects which today affect the residential project:

▶ its new programmatic definition, in syntony with various uses and forms of life undergoing accelerated change.

▶ its new spatial and technical definition, in complicity with new instrumental knowledge and the consequent optimization of the means referred to above.

▶ **AND LASTLY, ITS NEW PROJECTURAL INSERTION IN CONTEMPORARY SPACE AND ITS ULTIMATE POTENTIAL FOR SYNERGY WITH THE SPECIFIC NOTION OF THE CITY.**

5. 'Starting from [this] new multiplicity (...) contemporary criticism can [simply] undertake the construction of maps, of descriptions that, as in topographical charts, display the complexity of a territory, the resulting form of agencies (...) silently confronting a seemingly immobile mass, but which is riven by currents, flows, changes and interactions provoking incessant mutations.' Cf. SOLÀ-MORALES, Ignasi: *Diferencias. Topografía de la arquitectura contemporánea*, Editorial G.G., Barcelona, 1995.

Our loans are so easy, we're practically handing over your dream home.

2

COMMERCIAL, UNIVERSAL, TRIVIAL

In its day, the exhibition and catalog 'International Property', put together by Yago Conde and Bea Goller,[6] offered—via a selection of press announcements and messages taken from the global mass media—a meditation on the real-estate phenomenon and its influence on the construction of the territory: as a consequence, housing was shown, antonomastically, to be the 'product'. A market asset wholly inserted within the mechanisms of consumer society and thereby subject to commercial forces mainly inclined towards the generalization—and trivialization—of messages: common standards of a universal kind (a nostalgia for the rural, the caricaturing of comfort, an evocation of the atemporal...) directed towards the most deep-rooted, stable and permanent aspects of the collective imagery.

Codes shared, surprisingly enough, on a planetary scale by a nebulous 'middle class' that would have transformed its desires into an 'elemental and abstract system of ideologies.'[7]

GEORGE RITZER describes this generalized phenomenon perfectly, defining it as 'A MACDONALDSIZATION OF SOCIETY AND CONSUMPTION',[8] based on four basic standards: efficacy (a direct relation between appetite and satisfaction), cost-effectiveness (a seemingly sound product, yet cheap), predictability (an identifiable, recognizable, familiar image) and control (order, repetition and a convincing 'asepticism').

HAVING SAID THAT, THE THEME OF HOUSING CONTINUES TO BE A SPHERE PARTICULARLY GIVEN TO CONVENTIONALISM, to the repetition (on the part of private and also, ultimately, public promoters) of archetypes accommodated in the safe standards of an ambiguous, eclectic and obstinately conservative 'neolanguage' (even in moments like the present, where it appears to awaken a clear desire within the discipline for a theoretical repositing of the subject).[9]

A 'SCLEROSIS' WHICH NOT ONLY ALLUDES TO SUCH MERELY SPECULATIVE SCHEMES, BUT ALSO FREQUENTLY TO THOSE WHICH, TO USE A COMMONLY ACCEPTED EXPRESSION, WOULD TEND TO BE THOUGHT OF AS 'REFINED'. AND THE LATTER CONTINUES, IN EFFECT, TO BE A PARTICULARLY WEIGHTY ISSUE FOR OUR RECENT PAST.

The chosen refuge of those revisionist dogmas so in vogue a few years ago, built around a sacralized 'architecture of the city' and centered on the 'recovery of memory' as a reaction to the anathemized rupture—both semantic and spatial—that modernity supposed. A line consecrated by a certain, still actively belligerent disciplinary culture, which would seek its principal source of inspiration in urban models founded on tradition.

Ⓐ Back-to-back housing, three images
- Modern (standardization)
- Postmodern (evocation)
- Contemporary (combination)
1. Docomomo Archive
2. Lars Tubjörk, from *Landet, Utom Sij*, 1991
3. W.J. Neutelings. Hollainhof (Ghent 1995-97). Manipulated collage

Ⓑ Robot portrait of the 'House of Our Dreams' *El País Dominical* 8/1/95

---

6. Cf. 'International Property', in the collection *Quaderns Monografies*, COAC, Barcelona, 1995. Catalogue of the exhibition of the same name conceived by the architects Yago Conde and Bea Goller (January 1995).
7. Cf. VAN DER TOORN, Roemer: 'Archaisme, Fascinisme, Réflexivité,' in *Europan III*, op. cit.
8. Cf. RITZER, George: *Le McDonalización de la sociedad*, Ariel, Barcelona, 1996
9. As demonstrated in the conferences on 'Arquitectura y Vivienda' recently organized in Spain (Valencia 1992, Seville 1995, Oviedo 1996, Zaragoza 1996), outstanding among which was that organized by the COAV through 1995 under the title 'Nuevos Modos de Habitar', coordinated by the architect María MELGAREJO. Cf. the anthology of texts published on the occasion as a catalogue/book, *Nuevos Modos de habitar*, COAC, Valencia, 1996.

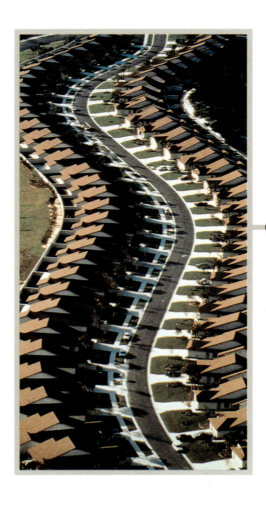

©

Ⓓ
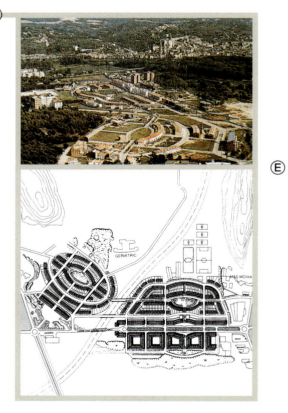
Ⓔ

Models primarily built around the basic idea of continuity and repetition
(be it typological, constructional, grammatical, of design, of image, of usage...)
inherited from a time characterized by the sloth and gradualness of change
and underpinned, principally, by three ancient myths:
- Confidence in a historical model of the city in which housing appears
as the principal generator—and figurative support—of the fabric
(THE STREET AS CENTRAL EVENT).
- Confidence in the persistence of an eternal coherence between type and
building (TECHNIQUE AS PROCEDURAL TRADITION).
- Interest in the 'typological' as the translation of a certain 'common habit'
(HOUSING AS ARCHETYPE).

The permanence, in sum, of various assumed 'invariants' (of typology,
morphology, design, construction...) capable of referring any intervention
to a metaphysical 'communion with context'.

For most of the past two decades this has been, in effect, the first objective
of official urbanism: namely the 'recuperation' or 'recreation' of an urban
space of traditional outlines whose 'recomposition' would have been entrusted
principally to a pragmatic 'caretaker' urbanism based on the strict control
of urban processes and on the alleged infallibility of the computer drawing:
NOSTALGIC PLANNING as a compositional intention, as a primarily figurative
act oriented towards the reconstruction of the fabric or, in the new
development of outlying areas, towards its recreation: models derived from
an archaizing concept of the urban, in which a picturesque and rememorative
historical center would coexist with a halo of surrounding
mini-arcades, caricatures of the garden-city or quaint neo-suburbs wholly
indebted to a certain pseudo-refined and pseudo-vernacular imagery, still
trusting in the efficacy of those apparently essential parameters
of architectonic discourse (geometric plans, axial layouts, symmetrical
compositions, 'solid' constructions). Neo-monumental forms and orders
solemnly imposed on the landscape and founded on the recreation of
old standards of historical urbanism (the enclosed city block, the picturesque
'coping', the classical crescent...) as disciplinary stereotypes.

Supposedly 'respectful' attitudes, materialized in an assumed formal neutrality
('accessible' building techniques, clichéd distributive solutions 'conveniently'
reinterpreted, and above all a generalized figurative uniformity) designed
to traduce a desire for 'control' and a syntactical discretion based,
fundamentally, on the soundness of the already-tried.

**FORCE OF HABIT AND MISCONSTRUED PRAGMATISM STILL TEND TO
INSPIRE THOSE TYPES OF UNDERTAKING BASED ON THE UTILIZATION OF
ENDOGENOUS CONVENTIONS**, which, accepted in advance, no longer
seem to respond to any stimulus except perhaps
the one provided by those old clichés of sentimental atavism, even if they
are still momentarily viable from the economic or political point of view. Codes
trusting in the 'certified guarantee' of old models and in the apparent stability
and permanence of decision-making but which, however, present ever-greater
difficulties when measured against a reality that is much more complex, rapid
and incoherent, conditioned by upheaval and **CHANGE**, and destined to
contradict, time and again, any anecdotic dream of order and harmony.

These are **CHANGES WHICH AFFECT THE VERY NOTION OF 'TIME' ITSELF**:
a time which, as **YORGOS SIMEOFORIDIS**[10] points out, is no longer one of
gradual and repetitive duration—that comforting time of the 'myth and narrative'
of the classical city—but an arythmic time, consisting of jolts, expulsions,
surprises and intertwinings; a time of ephemeral and disconcerting durations,
and inescapably demystifying by virtue of the constant sensation of perceptual
perplexity and questioning which characterizes the contemporary mind, one
completely open to the presence of the unwonted, of the artificial.

© 'Snakes' and 'Swimming Pools'. Reproduced from 'L.A. Patterns' (Progressive Architecture)

Ⓓ 'South Madrid' growth area, 1994. Reproduced from The New Suburbs of Madrid, Municipal Urban Management Department, Madrid City Council, 1995

Ⓔ The Fontajau neighborhood (Girona). Institut Català del Sòl, 1991

10. Cf. SIMIEOFORIDIS, Yorgos: 'Transitions,' in Europan III, op. cit.

▶ CHANGES, ALSO, IN THE WIDER SETTING ITSELF, no longer amenable to civic, domestic, liturgical bucolicism, but rather to the forcefulness of 'non-places'[11], the constant mutability of marginal spaces, the stridency of quotidian landscapes; a space of relationship and detachment—all at the same time—, of coexistence and estrangement; a space subject to new rituals (be they commercial, ludic or media-related) in which things tend to become 'near' and simultaneously 'far', 'known' and 'surprising', banal (through media saturation) and suggestive (through being unforeseen, recent).

▶ CHANGES, LASTLY, IN THE WAY OF LIFE ITSELF, which reveal themselves (and equally in the architectonic responses made to them) to be sensitive to the current heterogeneity of spatial experience and to that diffuse mixing of the everyday and the extraordinary, the predictable and the surprising, which tends to increasingly articulate experience and behavior, given the increasing role that the new information and data-processing technologies, and the media, tend to play in work and domestic life. NEW WAYS OF LIFE affected by many external agents, among the most significant manifestations of which one might note[12]

▶ the transformation of the 'family unit', with a predominance of couples without children or with few children. The progressive substitution of the classical notion of 'coexistence'—shared behavior—for that of a 'cohabitation'—a merely spatial contract (or relationship)—capable of favoring the independence of both varied kinds of action and behavior and changing individual needs;

▶ the growing sensibilization towards marginal collectives (the focal points of poverty, homeless individuals, refugees, underdeveloped regions, etc). But also a new consciousness of a type of wandering domestic life increasingly disseminated throughout the city: the substitution of private space by a diffused space of services at the urban level (bars, restaurants, launderettes, sports clubs, leisure centers, etc.) in a city converted into an enormous 'dispersed dwelling' for a nomadic user;

▶ the constant fluctuation of the labor market and the associated feeling of the instability of any work, with the consequent difficulty of long-term economic planning, and thus of automatic access to privately-owned housing; and the acceptance, then, of a change of paradigm linked which would favor progressive acceptance of the idea of mobility, of a greater reversibility in decision-making and an increase in rentable housing, etc.;

▶ and lastly, the increasing 'joint-participation' of the active members in the family economy, and thus the need for reducing domestic tasks, which would favor a new concept of those service spaces (kitchen and bathroom) leading to their conversion, in certain cases, into truly ludic areas ('bathroom-gymnasium' or 'kitchen-laboratory') with an increasing technological input.

In short, to understand the house, as ELIA ZENGHELIS AND ELENI GIGANTES[13] suggest, as a place closer to the lifestyle of 'leisure' and 'comfort' than to the habitual 'austerity' of a space thought of as mere 'social necessity': a 'new housing' planned, in fine, from the point of view of diversity and individuality rather than homogeneity and collectivity.

All these are indices of an evolution in social habits which allow us to point to new concepts in the approach to the contemporary habitat: new concepts in the design of the lived space itself (the residential cell and the interior landscape given over to it), but also new concepts in the definition of those new support systems (and hence of the relational landscapes associated with them) capable of guaranteeing a workable and renewed relationship between housing, city and territory.

TWO FIELDS—INTERIOR AND EXTERIOR LANDSCAPE—WHICH WOULD ALLUDE, AT ALL EVENTS, TO THE ACTUAL REDEFINITION OF RESIDENTIAL SPACE, AND WHICH WOULD, IN THE LAST ANALYSIS, BE CALLED ON TO COMBINE WITH IT.

11. Cf. COSTA, Xavier: 'No-llocs i metròpoli,' in Quaderns 207-208-209, 1995.
12. For further development of this theme, expressed during a round table, cf. 'Vivienda: nuevas alternativas,' in Quaderns 210, 1995.
13. Cf. GIGANTES, Elleni & ZENGHELIS, Elia: 'Conversaciones,' in El Croquis 67.

Domestic settings, global settings
1. The 'Ringcultuur'. (from. Vlees en Beton. Rotterdam, 1988)
2. Chauncy Hare. West Chester Pennsylvania, 1971

Non-places of leisure and consumerism
3. Gasworks Park (Richard Haag Architects, Seattle, 1975)

The everyday and the extraordinary
4. Televiewer (Photo: Lars Tunbjörk, Ölans 1991)
5. New housing in the Old Town. V. Guallart, 1991 (cf. Quaderns 203)
6. Connected workers (archive photo)

Images of limits, images of artifice
7. Sports fish. Advertising image
8. Razor blade. Advertising image
9. 'Antennas'. Archive image

Solitary urbanite, nomadic urbanite
10. Homeless vehicle (K. Wodiczko, 1989) (in Ottogono 97, 1990)
11. Toyo Ito. Nomad woman (Tokyo, 1985-86)
12. Renée Kool. Catharsis (Utrecht 1993)

Mixed settings, denaturalized settings
13. Kitchen-office (archive photo)
14. Hotel-office (archive photo)
15. Bali in Florence (Photo: Martin Parr, El País 1995)

Ⓐ Clinical sections
1. Hierarchized (classical) structure (section through a Haussmann-period Paris house, 1853)
2. Obsolete (postmodern) structure (photomontage based on a residential building in Lausanne, *Fenêtres habitées*, Architekturmuseum, Basel 1989)
3. Polyvalent (contemporary) structure ('Domus Demain', architect: Yves Lyon, 1984)

INTERIOR LANDSCAPE: 'INHABITED UNITS' AND THE RESIDENTIAL CELL

The concept of the residential cell has been limited, traditionally, to the appointing of an ideal partitioning between two floors: layout-types—founded on the idea of typology and set out according to the systematized schemes of *Existenzminimum*—understood as elemental units capable of being repeated *ad infinitum* on a ground plan.

In his book *Inhabited Windows*,[14] **ROGER DIENER** demonstrates (using studies made by the students of the Lausanne School of Architecture that, by means of clinical sections through the old residential buildings in the city center, allow the diversity of ways of life that co-exist in a single—and obsolete—stratified reality to be revealed) **THE GENERALIZED COLLAPSE OF ANY YEARNING FOR A RESIDENTIAL STEREOTYPE**: the heterogeneity confronting that clonic family which seems to go on inspiring the majority of current interventions and norms, based generally on the scheme of 'a living room-dining room-kitchen-utility room-bathroom-cloakroom' and three or four bedrooms, and all in '90 square meters', as a commonly accepted formula.

The majority of recent research projects today argue—as do **MONIQUE ELEB VIDAL, ANNE-MARIE CHÂTELET AND THIERRY MANDOUL** in their book *Penser l'habité*[15]—for the advisability of **DELVING DEEPER INTO THE REDEFINITION OF INHABITED SPACE, STARTING FROM A GREATER POLYFUNCTIONING AND POLYVALENCE OF SPACES, AS WELL AS THE EVENTUAL COHABITATION OF VARIOUS SUBTYPES, IN HAPPY COMBINATION; PARAMETERS WHICH ALLUDE, IN ANY EVENT, TO A STRATEGIC ARTICULATION BETWEEN USAGE, TECHNIQUE AND SPACE.**

14. Cf. DIENER, Roger, with BARBEY, G., JEHLE, U. & STRAUSS, S.: *Fenêtres habitées*, Architekturmuseum, Basle, 1989.
15. Cf. ELEB VIDAL, Monique, CHÂTELET, Anne-Marie & MANDOUL, Thierry: *Penser l'habité: le logement en question*, Pierre Mardaga, Liège, 1988.

Ⓑ A thousand windows: the new privacy
1. Llinars del Vallès. Photo: Jordi Bernadó (architects: Frutos, Sanmartin, Valor 1995) (*Quaderns* 210, 1995)
2. Bordeaux 1994. Photo: J. Chiomoff. (reproduced from *Résidence-joyeuse à Bordeaux*, Europan-Untimely Books, Athens, 1994)
3. Jean-Luc Godard's *Tout va bien*, 1973
4. 'The New Private Realm,' in *The Berlage Cahiers* 3 (1993-94). Éditions 010, Rotterdam 1995

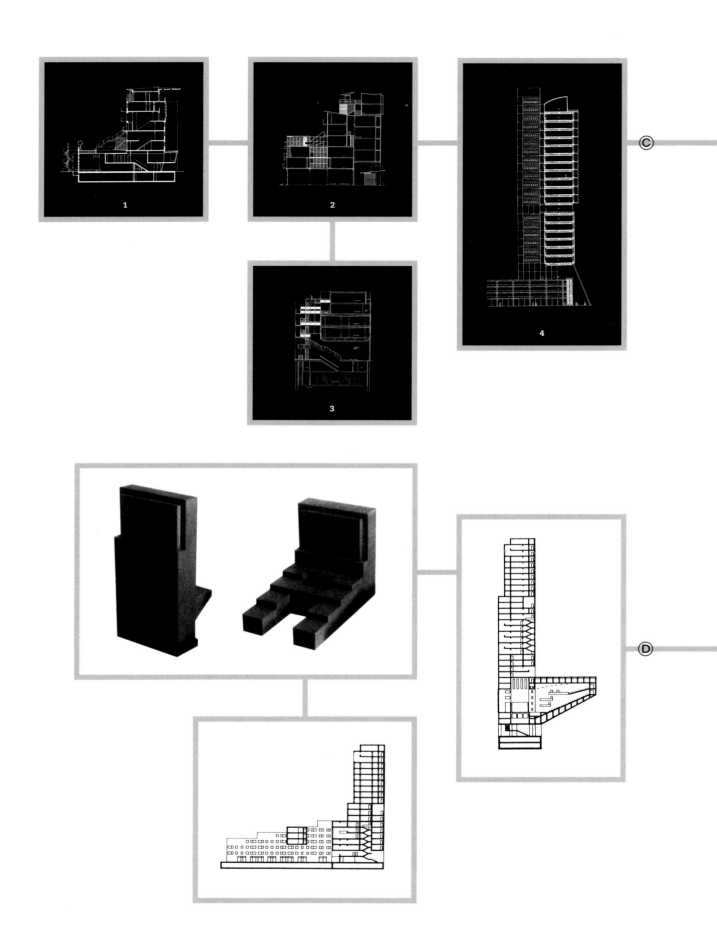

3.1. DIVERSITY rather than repetition

Diversity understood as combinatory possibility liable to favor a productive mixing together of many types and programs proceeding from the concept of new mechanisms and more polyvalent processes.

▶ THE WORK IN MIXED SECTIONS IS SHOWN TO BE AN EXPLICIT FORM OF ACTION AT THE MOMENT OF PLANNING FOR A DIVERSITY WHICH IS NOT ONLY HORIZONTAL BUT ALSO VERTICAL,

a diversity which would coincide, moreover, with the increasing coexistence of the residence with other heterogeneous activities, accumulative in height through the utilization of ever less determinate structural systems (with greater spans, for example, than those used hitherto in residential models).
The complex sections of the programmatic building planned by **MATHIAS SAUERBRUCH AND ELIA ZENGHELIS** for Checkpoint Charlie (Berlin, 1992) or **DUWENSEE-KREPLIN**'s 'urban megaforms' for Rostock (1992) and the hybrid buildings by **JEAN NOUVEL** in Tours (1995) and **ÁBALOS-HERREROS** in Barcelona (1990) illustrate this interest for combining high-rise programs and types. As opposed to the ancient type-structure pairing, the evolution of current techniques permits a greater structural indeterminacy (thus overcoming the old servitude to five-meter bays and partitioning constrained to a narrow space between two walls). The amplification of longitudinal spans calls, in certain cases, for longitudinal development parallel to the façade (in blocks of narrow bands) rather than transversal development in depth, favoring fascia of a more diaphanous and illuminated style which permit the appearance of complementary 'non-concrete' places (interior/exterior galleries, semi-patios, covered terraces, etc.).

▶ A DIVERSITY, IN OTHER CASES, FOLLOWING ON FROM THE IMPLEMENTATION OF ELEMENTAL SCHEMES BASED ON THE DISPOSITION OF FIXED ELEMENTS AND VARIABLE SPACES,

through the strategic positioning of service cores (sanitation, kitchens, technical installations, etc.), and the variable 'modelling' of a single and fluid space defined by them.
Basic devices—like those conceived by **HERZOG & DE MEURON** in Pulvermühle (Berlin, 1993), **RIEGLER & RIEWE** in Graz-Strassgang (Graz, 1991-94), **MORGER-DEGELO** in Kleinbasel (Basle, 1994) or the **ACTAR** team in its projects for Buitrago de Lozoya (Madrid, 1989-91), and primarily by Calella (Barcelona, 1992), Son Gibert (Majorca, 1993) and Graz (1996), using the so-called 'ABC System'—would allow the creation of a wide range of solutions largely based on strategic movements of 'concentration' in the service spaces—equipped 'coagula' or 'clots' thought of as 'hard cores'—and in the variable growth (yet in accordance with the precision of elementary 'guideline' systems) of the other fields, in successive combinations which, through the variable rhythm of the dividing elements, would encourage the appearance of distinct subtypes with various superficial margins.[16]

© Mixed sections
1. 'Checkpoint Charlie' building (architects: Sauerbruch-Zengelis, Berlin 1992)
2. 'Double-block' building (architects: Brunet-Béal, Barcelona H/C, 1990)
3. 'Combi' building (architect: Jean Nouvel, Tours 1995)
4. 'Multi-use' building (architects: Abalos-Herreros, Barcelona H/C, 1990)

© 'Hybrid megaforms' (Duwensee-Kreplin, Rostock, 1992)

16. Véase ELEB VIDAL, CHATELET & MANDOUL: 'La flexibilidad como dispositivo,' in *Quaderns* 202, 1993.

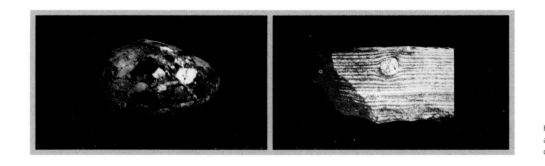

Hard nuclei–nodes, lumps and surrounding areas of development and dilation

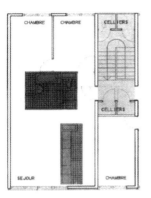 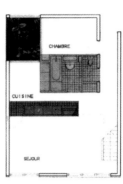 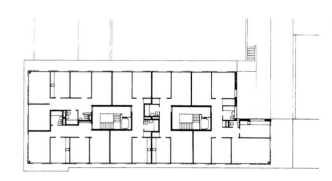

↰ Lacoste-Robain.
60 dwellings,
Épinay-sur-Seine
(Paris 1993)

Morger Degelo.
26 dwellings
(Kleinbasel, 1994).
Creation of a subtype
from the movement–
gyration of the
bathroom nuclei

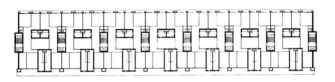 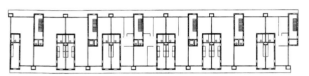

↰ Herzog & de Meuron.
Pulvermühle (Berlin
1993). Service spaces
as coagula

Herzog & de Meuron.
Variation of an identical
range of possibilities

 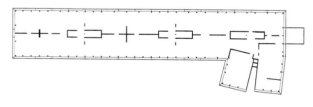

Actar Arquitectura
(with Montserrat Torras).
34 housing units
(Madrid 1991).
Combinatory scheme
based on fixed nuclei
and variable growths

 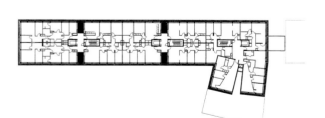

Francis Soler.
Residential building
in Bercy. Structural
organization and
potential distribution

Comparative study in plan of various schemes employing typological diversity
and spatial flexibility. Most of the projects are planned
as combinatory systems using variable elements: fixed modules and nodes repeated
in varying rhythms and engendering variable rhythms–subtypes–of growth

ACTAR Arquitectura (with Arenas-Basiana). 300 housing units (Majorca 1993). A, B, C module type and combinatory schema based on identical surfaces and different spatial organizations.

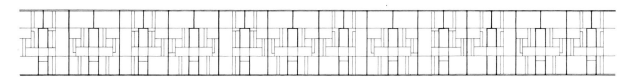

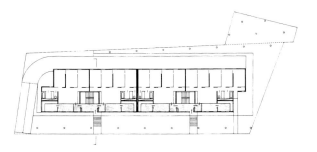

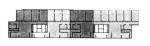
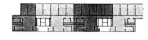

Njiric & Njiric. Housing units (Graz 1993). Schema and variations. Fixed nuclei and variable growths based on a border of flexible use in the façades and isotropic divisions in the rooms.

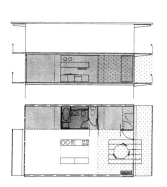

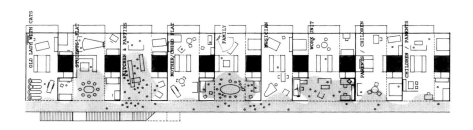

Njiric & Njiric. Housing units (Den Bosch, 1993). A fixed module and combinatory schemas based on fixed nuclei and variable growths.

HOUSING: TWO COMBINATORY SYSTEMS

ABC system

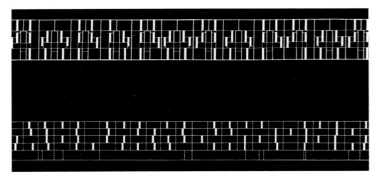

Combinatory grid (plan and elevation)

Different ground plan combinations

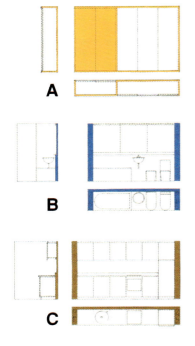

Equipped walls–ABC unitary elements
Cupboard/accumulator
- Bathroom/kitchen

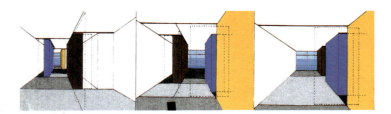

Interior landscapes with colored monoliths

Architects:
ACTAR ARQUITECTURA
Manuel Gausa,
Aureli Santos,
Oleguer Gelpí
Ignasi Pérez Arnal
Florence Raveau
1994

Ground plan as combinatory system

The ABC system approaches the possibility of generating different subtypes on the basis of the movement of service nuclei in a previously-defined, set surface unit (approximately 70 sqm): a space with a double facade, 5.5 meters wide and 14 meters deep.
The proposal is based on the variable siting of three prefabricated equipped walls, following the ABC formula (in Spanish: Armario, Baño, Cocina; storage space, bathroom, kitchen), conceived as hard elements (coagula, clusters) in a surrounding fluid space, the elimination of interior partitioning and its substitution by sliding panels being favored. The changeable position of the modules responds to an elemental guideline of functional strips which cross-hatches the technical decking of each floor, as in a musical stave. Different combinations appear here which encompass more conventional layouts (based on two or three bedrooms) and other more open ones of the 'loft' type.
In the facade the expressive, variable manifestation of each one of the modules elicits a varied rhythm of vertical edges of different colors, combined with the designed facings (glazed, opaque, fixed or sliding and protective) which act as enclosures.

RAIL system

Combinatory grid (plan and elevation)

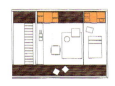

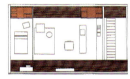

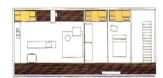

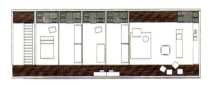

Different ground plan dimensions and combinations

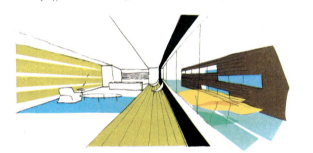

Interior landscapes (rooms as 'localities')

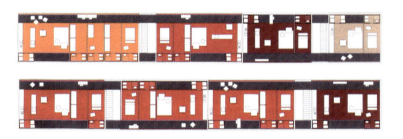

Ground plan as combinatory system

The notion of 'thick wall' and 'filter facade leads to the gradual concentration of service spaces in peripheral strips (party walls or, in this case, facades), prompting greater versatility of the inner space.
In the Rail system, the interior distribution and organization follows three functional, lengthwise strips. The first and most open, running along the south-facing facade, is conceived as an ambiguous space. A mixture of corridor, gallery and recreational filter–for relaxation– between inside and out. The main living functions (bedrooms, lounge, etc.) are set in the broad central strip. Privacy inside each of the rooms is ensured by large, light, roller blinds. The strip which runs along the more closed facade houses a free arrangement of service nuclei (bathrooms, dressing rooms, small study spaces, etc.). This simple, functional distribution allows for great flexibility of solution and type. Its application to the facade itself (also defined by the combination of various overlapping strips of different materials and sizes) ensures a varied, direct arrangement according to the different solutions adopted in the ground plan.

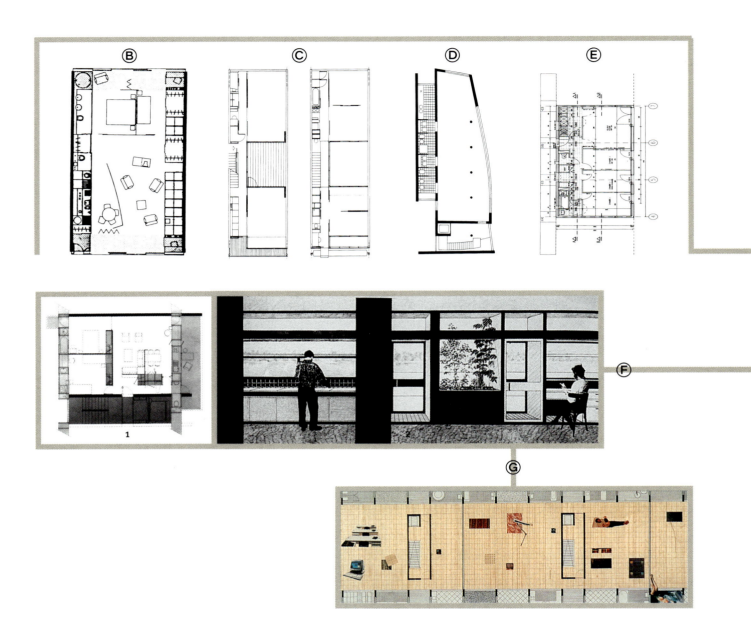

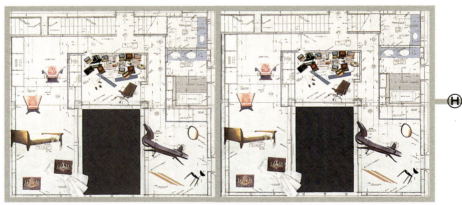

28

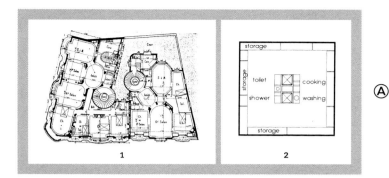

Ⓐ Ground plan composition versus ground plan system
1. Composite layout of rooms in a classical building (Paris 1907)
2. Contemporary spatial indeterminacy (S. Gansell. House for nomads (1994) (*The Berlage Cahiers*, 3 1995)

3. 2. EMPTIED-OUT rather than partitioned-off

The new structural changes permit a progressive freeing of the interior space (thought of as a large technical floor) and the concentration of the service spaces in increasingly peripheral functional bands. The definition of the party wall, no longer as a simple dividing line but as a 'technical width', a 'thick wall' or transversal 'service wall', would allow for solutions based on functional transparent fascia like those used by **DELSALLE-LAUCOURDRE** in their 'Nouveau Habitat' project (PAN 14, 1988), **BÉAL-BRUNET** in their housing for the Avenida Diagonal (Barcelona, 1990), **LACOSTE-ROBAIN** in his Rue Partants housing (Paris, 1992) and **NEUTELINGS-DE KOONING** in their loft-building (Amberes, 1993).
The use of the facade, no longer as a simple 'interior/exterior' dividing line, but as an effective services support, an alveolar thickness (or 'filter facade') of equipped or empty superfluities, which allow light and air to penetrate—just as **YVES LION AND NEUTELINGS-WALL-DE GEYTER-ROODBEEN** propose, respectively, in their projects 'Domus Demain' (1984) and H/C (Barcelona, 1990)—would also encourage the formalization of continuous fascia of facilities designed to accommodate the system's fixed elements and so free the rest of the space, thus reclaiming 'the idea of the loft, locus of all possibility.'
Both the 'Six Memos' scheme conceived by **NJIRIC & NJIRIC** and the 'RAIL' system planned by **ACTAR** for their Aubervilliers project (Paris, 1996) employ similar devices, proceeding from the organization of the cell in various widths, 'bar codes' intended to encourage optional uses and installations through the functional optimization of the perimetral fascias. Just as the city is no longer a nexus of harmoniously grouped elements, so housing ceases to be a nexus of meticulously distributed rooms and becomes a '**SPACE INTENDED FOR HABILITATION'; A SPACE DEFINED FROM A FUNCTIONAL PERIPHERY AND MANIFESTED AS AN EMPTINESS 'TO BE APPROPRIATED'**. The construction and the fittings, with services grouped as volumes, thus form the most stable frame: the rest may eventually introduce itself into the ambit of the temporal, the mobile, the polyvalent.[17]

17. Cf. ELEB VIDAL, CHÂTELET & MANDOUL: 'La flexibilidad como dispositivo', in *Quaderns* 202, 1993.

Technical party walls

Ⓑ Delsalle-Laucoudre. Nouveau Habitat Pan 1º (1988). Technical party walls

Ⓒ Béal-Brunet. Nouveau Habitat–H/C Competition (Barcelona, 1990)

Ⓓ Neutelings-De Kooning. Loft in Antwerpen, 1993

Ⓔ Lacoste-Robain. (41 P.L.S. housing units, Paris 1992)

Service facades

Ⓕ 1 & 2. Yves Lion. 'Domus Demain' (1984)

Ⓖ W.J. Neutelings, A. Wall, X. de Geyter, F. Roodbeen. Dwelling type for the H/C Competition (Barcelona 1990)

Equipped spaces
Ⓗ OMA. Housing units in Fukuoka (1991).

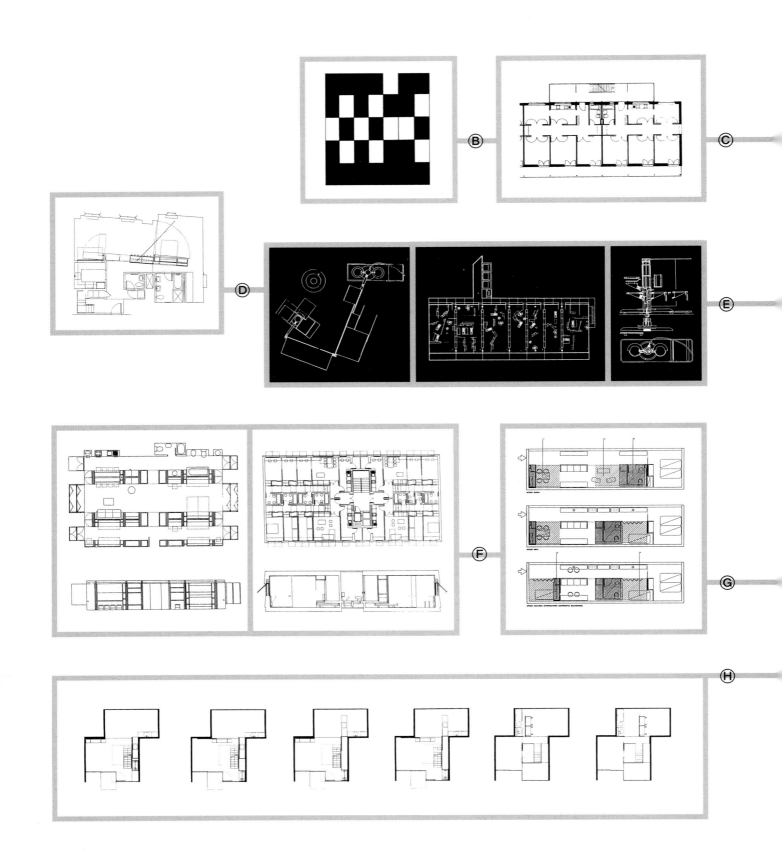

Ⓐ Furniture as accumulator, furniture as that which determines form
1. 'Equipped' multipurpose cupboard
2. Designed multipurpose cupboard (A. Wexler, Small Buildings)
3. Functional cupboard (A. Wexler, Small Buildings)

3. 3. FLEXIBILITY rather than specialization

The new conception of flexibility (going beyond the caricature of the handyman user dedicated to continually transforming the interior of his house) must be associated today with the idea itself of the polyvalence and versatility of space. Equally important in that sense would be both tactical interventions of a structural order (the increasing use of large spans and the minimization of the structure) or those related to the idea of fittings (a strategic concentration of technical modules, a planned appointing of energy supplies, emptied out) and those referring to more or less evolutive layout and partitioning systems. ALL THIS TO ARRIVE AT A GREATER ISOTROPY AND SPATIAL INDETERMINACY. Based at first sight on a simple, conventional partitioning of rooms, the 'flexibility-serialization-repetition' nexus would lead, for example, to a more isotropic space being imagined, by means of the appointing of rooms sufficiently similar in size as to be functionally non-determinant, thus favoring various changes in occupancy and use, as in a virtual checkerboard.[18] The possibility of favoring a more fluid and transformative space would encourage the investigation, elsewhere, of systems of evolutive partitioning; systems based, for preference, on mass-produced or industrialized elements—sliding, folding and collapsable panels, technical fittings, swivelling units, dismountable ceilings or partitions, etc. Likewise, the use in office layout of 'cloisons épaisses' (thick partitions), usual when creating separate, reversible spaces with storage capacity (generally based on modules of 60 x 60 x 204), also permits the creation of solutions adapted to the importance of the 'accumulative' factor (storerooms, cupboards, shelving) and substituted for the classical divider partition, as well as restoring the notion of the 'threshold' between spatial fields.

And the old idea of the container (a large chest or cupboard) as a furniture-object 'deposited' in the space (but also as a reconvertible, transformable piece) suggests various possibilities, when favoring a continuous rearrangement of the space. Convertible technical fittings or moveable objects play, in that open and fluid virtual space, the same role as traditional dividing panels, but with greater versatility of use. The multipurpose nuclei of the 'H/C' project of ÁBALOS-HERREROS (1990) or the transformable service units planned by ARANGUREN-GALLEGOS for Leganés and Venta-Berri (1995) and by JOSÉ MANUEL BARRERA in his design for evolutive housing (Valencia, 1995), are some examples of this polyvalent treatment of a multiform and atypical space, possible today thanks to the existence of technical solutions already tried out in the tertiary sector: equipped planes and connecting networks of installations in registrable surfaces permit the elasticity of a space open to further possibilities. 'UNIVALENT' SPACE THUS GIVES WAY TO A 'MULTIVALENT' SPACE WHICH IS MADE UP OF SUCCESSIVE, REVERSIBLE 'SUB-SPACES'.[19]

Ⓑ Xaveer de Geyter. Scheme for an interwoven ideogram for Borneo Sporenburg (1995)

Ⓒ Kuhn-Pfiffner. Housing units in Lenzburg (1993-94). Repetition of functionally non-differentiated units

Ⓓ Smith Miller-Hawkinson. Apartment in New York (1989) cf. *Quaderns* 202

Ⓔ Ábalos-Herreros. (Barcelona 1990). Housing units on the Diagonal. Peripheral concentration of services and evolutive furniture

Ⓕ Aranguren-Gallegos. 200 housing units in Leganés (1994). General plan and section (cf. *Quaderns* 211)
2. Aranguren-Gallegos. 180 housing units in Venta Berri (1994). General plan and section (cf. *Quaderns* 211)

Ⓖ José Manuel Barrera. (Valencia 1995). Evolutive housing

Ⓗ R. Gómez Moriana. Ideal Double Standard (1994). Convertible housing unit (*The Berlage Cahiers* 3, 1995)

18. Cf. 'Vivienda: nuevas alternativas,' op. cit., especially the interventions of Pere Joan Ravetllat and Jordi Garcés.
19. Cf. ELEB VIDAL et al., 1993, op. cit.

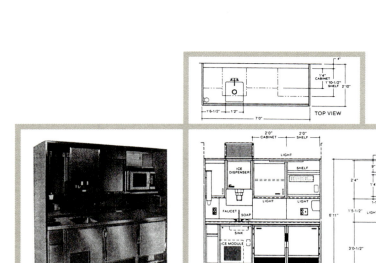
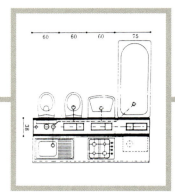
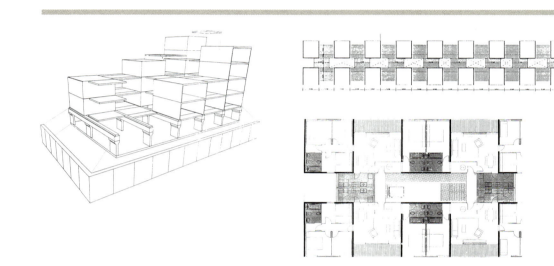

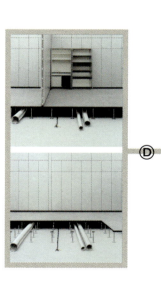

32

Ⓐ Industrialization rather than handicraft
1. Show housing for Incasol (Fontajau neighborhood, Girona 1991)
2. Némausus (architect: Jean Nouvel) Nîmes 1989

3.4. INDUSTRIALIZATION rather than handicraft:

Faced with the oft-claimed suitability of quasi-artisanal methods and technologies which are cumbersome and also expensive to use, an alternative—and eventually more effective—solution would in effect consist in

THE EXPLORATION AND INTEGRATION OF THOSE TECHNIQUES, MATERIALS AND PRODUCTS COMMON IN OTHER INCREASINGLY DEVELOPED SECTORS

(the tertiary sector, industry, consumerism) but hitherto underused—if not rejected outright—by traditional residential design and construction. Solutions which, furthermore, would allow a greater precision, versatility, speed and efficiency to be achieved in the construction process:

▶ On the one hand, one might point to the growing importance of basically **SEMI-PREFABRICATED** systems (not a 'hard' prefabrication oriented towards the repetition of complete cellular modules, but a 'tactical' prefabrication used both in the structure—frames and decks of basically pre-stressed sheets, usually of 9 x 2.4 m^2, for favoring potential mixed structures—and in the installations and fixtures, through the use of small technical units or, preferably, of so-called **'EQUIPPED WALLS'** which would include complete installations and fixtures, open to different spatial combinations.

▶ The further substitution of traditional heavy enclosures—based on damp and massive wall systems—by much lighter ones based on dry materials (metal 'sandwich' panels or multilayered wood-derived ones, with the subsequently increasing incorporation of cement-based, polycarbonate, and/or fibre 'composites', etc.) should also be considered. Following on from this, the treatment of the **FACADE AS A 'DOUBLE FILTER' LAYER**, with facing and joinery on its interior surface and the reclaiming of an interior/exterior 'transitional width' (protected by means of sliding shutters, panels or blinds), permits the external presence to be fitted with a light membrane designed to substitute the traditional built heaviness and aggressivity—solid walls perforated by small openings—for **A MORE EVANESCENT AND LESS AGGRESSIVE IMAGE WITHIN THE LANDSCAPE.**

Ⓑ Semi-prefabricated equipped walls. Catalog elements and processes

Ⓒ Evolutive mutation systems. Architect: Pich-Aguilera Archs-Ass Layout and mounting system using three-dimensional prefabricated modules and concrete slabs

Ⓓ Equipped and registrable floors and walls (catalog elements)

Ⓔ Facade as a 'double filter' layer. Details:
1. Henke-Schreieck (Vienna, 1995)
2. Mazelle-Manescau-Steeg (Bordeaux, 1994)
3. Riegler & Riewe (Graz, 1994)
4. Francis Soler (París-Bercy, 1997)

p. 34

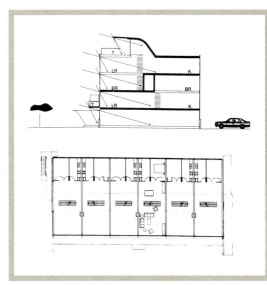

F

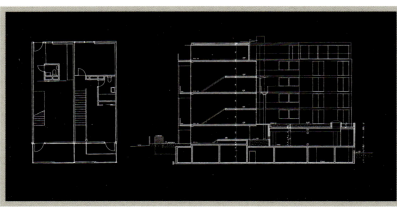

G

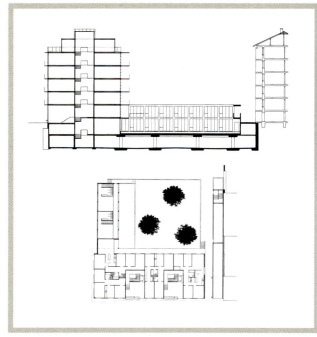

H

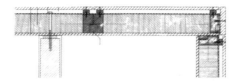

Morger-Degelo (Basel 1994). Mounting of the facade enclosures ('Eternit' prefabricated panels)

◗ Within this framework the exploration of systems of **SUSTAINABLE AIR CONDITIONING** should also be considered, beginning with the exterior incorporation of accumulating elements and the expressive optimization of those new materials of high inertia (metal sheeting, glass, polycarbonates, etc) in thermic facade widths.
The incorporation of **SYSTEMS SUITED TO THE NEW INSTALLATIONS** —registrable floors and false ceilings, etc—would be made compatible with a potential use of light structures for both storage and possible mezzanines (augmenting the usable height of the housing).
◗ Lastly, the growing importance of **THE IDEA OF RECYCLING** must be considered in this chapter: non-aggressive products, the re-utilization of means, low-impact construction, reversibility...
Frequently rejected simply out of considerations of image or procedural routine, these are some of the many procedures still to be explored, and which, furthermore, would permit a handling of residential construction much more in accord with the demands of the surroundings.
Pilot schemes like the now paradigmatic 'Némusus' operation of **JEAN NOUVEL** (Nîmes, 1989) would join with the other more recent ones presented later in this publication, like the housing buildings planned by **RIEGLER & RIEWE** (Graz, 1994), **MAZELLE-MANESCAU-STEEG** (Bordeaux, 1994), **MORGER-DEGELO** (Basel, 1994) or **FRANCIS SOLER** (Paris, 1997), or the well-known housing created by **JOSEP LLUIS MATEO** in Den Haag (1993) and Terrassa (1997), and by **DIETER HENCKE** and **MARTA SCHREIK** in Vienna (1995), all of which are more or less characteristic of this type of investigation.
Procedures, on the other hand, which would have, in the case of publically-promoted housing, a repercussion on construction costs, with a possible lowering of costs of around 10%, capable of permitting an eventual increase in interior surface area or a higher-quality finish. Possibilities tried out in experiments which remain embryonic, due more to inertia and market scepticism than to reasons of effectiveness.[20]

Josep Lluís Mateo (MAP Architects) Ⓕ The Hague (1993). View, section and plan. Construction based on prefabricated panels and slabs

"Dieter Hencke" & Maria Schreieck (Vienna 1995) Ⓖ Units with typological variations. The facade as double-layered enclosure

Morger Degelo (Basel 1994). Ⓗ Units with different subtypes. The facade as manifestation of variety
Photo: R. Walti

20. Cf. ÁBALOS & HERREROS: 'Construcción y vivienda: un posible decálogo,' in *Quaderns* 210, 1995.

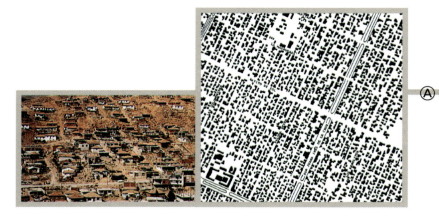 

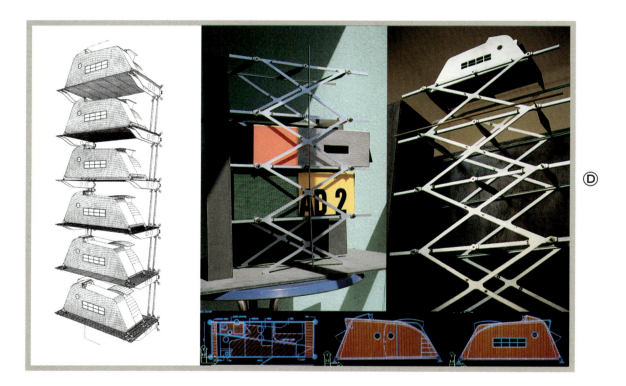

3.5. NEW CHALLENGES: solutions in emergency situations-projects for the renovation of obsolete structures

The need alluded to above for greater economy (both constructional and material), the potential reversibility of forms and uses in land (through the utilization of dry-assembly and disassembly schemes based on light structures) or the demand for easier housing access, understood as a personalized 'home' and not as a simple 'roof' or a mere statistical factor, signal a change of paradigm and the revision of many platitudes current up until now, going beyond the limits of old approaches (be they typological, sociological or semantic) to a subject too often considered from a position of conventional *a prioris*.

We are conscious today of the importance of the global phenomena of marginality, growth, massification and conflict, which customary disciplinary analyses of housing do not usually take into account. Phenomena around emergency situations determined, today, by other approaches to the habitat issue. On the one hand, it becomes increasingly necessary to resolve housing in the more developed countries in an appropriate and imaginative manner (attentive, then, to the particular characteristics of each set of problematics), and among those growing sectors of the population with nil or limited resources (pockets of poverty, transient immigrant populations, homeless groups, etc.). The skillful use of nonprofitable space (in both the landscape and the urban fabric: residual spaces, interstitial corners, narrow lots, breaches in the fabric, etc.) and the utilization of temporary structures of light construction, would permit—as in the case of the 'Butagaz plan' for the **DESIGN OF REFUGES FOR THE HOMELESS** promoted by **PAUL VIRILIO** in France—the generation of low-cost, high-quality public housing projects.[21]

HOWEVER, WE ARE CONSCIOUS TODAY THAT THE GREATEST HOUSING CRISIS DOES NOT EXIST IN THE PRECISELY MORE-DEVELOPED COUNTRIES, BUT IN 'THIRD-WORLD' COUNTRIES SUBJECTED TO VERTIGINOUS CHANGE AND EXPONENTIAL GROWTH,

one-fifth of the global population is located, today, in 'clandestine' human slums, spontaneous structures developed in destructured spaces, a consequence of rapid demographic increase and the general lack of economically-accessible housing.

Shanty towns, ghettos, suburbs of shacks go to form structures which are marginal to any order and planning; massified and conflictive conglomerations, but also, as **CHARLES CORREA** points out,[22] generators of new spatial responses to the issue of habitat which emerge directly out of the societies that have generated them. Self-organizing structures, then, which one might regard with an unprejudiced eye receptive to new stimuli.[23]

Self-organization processes

Ⓐ Mexico. Spontaneous occupancy
Photo: E. Ribbeck
(reproduced from *Daidalos* 50, 1993)

Ⓑ Aleppo, Syria. Self-built housing
Photo: E. Ribbeck
(reproduced from *Daidalos* 50, 1993)

Ⓒ Homeless vehicle (K. Wodiczko, 1980)

Ⓓ Willy Müller. Habitable structures of occupancy (1993-96)

21. Cf. 'Consulta Butagaz,' in *L'Architecture d'aujourd'hui*
22. Cf. CORREA, Charles: 'Comunicación UIA–Barcelona 96' in *Quaderns* 213, 1996.
23. Cf. KHAN MUMTAZ, Kamil: 'Comunicación UIA Barcelona 96,' Ibid.

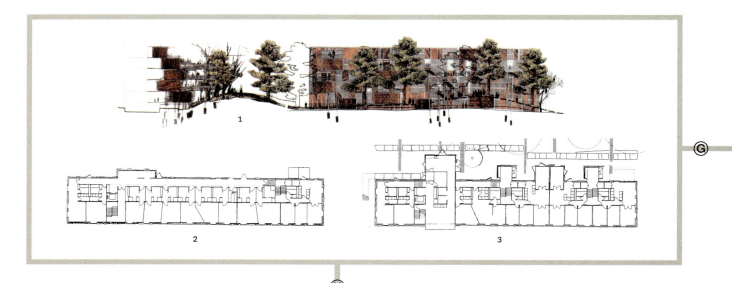

SPONTANEOUS MANIFESTATIONS RELATED TO THOSE OTHERS EMERGING OUT OF UNEXPECTED SITUATIONS OF CATASTROPHE or civil emergency (earthquakes, eruptions, floods, fire, armed conflicts...) which generate here, too, self-organizing and voluntary collective responses that compensate for an inefficient official machinery frequently paralyzed by lack of foresight. Situations which should duly be taken into account by civil organizations when it comes to designing workable solutions for the transfer, relocation and housing of transient populations, solutions requiring appropriate and adequate alternative systems for providing new habitational centers in areas of more or less temporary occupation.

Recognized in all these cases is the importance of working with a potential **'EPHEMERAL COLONIZATION' OF THE LANDSCAPE LINKED TO THE POSSIBILITY OF CONCEIVING REVERSIBLE SYSTEMS** of construction and occupation of the terrain; this suggests a potential reversal of the 'urbanizable' and the 'non-urbanizable', the stable and the temporal, and hence a revision of both the classic desire for 'residential property' and of the value of certain stretches of land related to it; the strategic allowance for certain 'areas of soft colonization', of low density and impact (in a state of temporary use and owned by nobody), would in effect permit the recycling of unused terrain, of scarce or nil real-estate value, but of undeniable environmental value (quarries, farming land, old re-used infrastructures, reclaimed space, etc.).

But the idea of recycling itself also introduces the necessity for thinking through fresh responses for other conflictive 'landscapes': those defined by the great residential schemes of the immediate postwar period.

An immense, rapidly-built real estate park, with obvious positive values, but also with important spatial, constructional and environmental pathologies, which today requires **DRASTIC OPERATIONS OF FUNCTIONAL SURGERY ON VARIOUS 'FABRICS' TOO RECENT TO BE SUFFICIENTLY VALUED,** yet already subject to clear signs of obsolescence. Residential estates, tourist megalopoles, dysfunctional outskirts would be some of the settings suitable for aid and reactivation projects—renovation schemes, in short—designed to halt ever-increasing processes of wear and tear and lack of adaptation, be these global interventions aimed at restructuring or simple epidermal schemes for that space of friction—the facade—generated between the building and its changing surroundings.

All this reflects the existence of a much deeper debate around the desire for 'preservation' and the need for 'intervention' in our medium (and the attendant preoccupation with forms of occupation, intervention and colonization in the territory and the landscape), already familiar from those more sensitized contexts.

These issues, however, cannot be pursued here. But it can be pointed out how, at this end of century, the renovation of the residential cell must grow out of its conception as support for a new perceptual experience capable of recapturing that 'exciting quality'[24] of a space made up of relationships, incidents and concatenations of plastic perception...

A landscape quality—be it the interior or exterior 'landscape'—destined to shift the debate on housing towards a particular reflection on contemporary urban space, on the decay, in fine, of the old 'city/territory' dichotomy which today rapidly forgoes some of its secular content and merges into ambiguous areas of tension, far from the comfortable parameters the discipline has used until the recent debate.

24. F. J. Barba Corsini dixit. Cf. the round table "Vivienda: nuevas alternativas", op. cit.

Ⓔ Rehousing in disaster areas
1. Kobe earthquake (*Kobe After the Earthquake*, Telescope, 1995)
2. Emergency housing, *Kobe*
1-2 photo: R. Miyamoto (*Kobe*, ed. Telescope. Tokyo, 1995
3. Temporary structures in devastated fabrics

Reversible structures in the landscape
Ⓕ Actar Arquitectura. 'M'house' prefabricated modules (1997).
The 'Flintstone' option: temporary occupancy in an inhabited quarry

Renovating
Ⓖ Architects: François Roche DSV & Sie. Renovation of an obsolete built structure (Sarcelles 1994)
1. Elevation and section
2. Ground floor and type

Renovating
Ⓗ Christian de Portzamparc. Rehabilitation of a group of buildings in the Rue Nationale (Paris 1993)

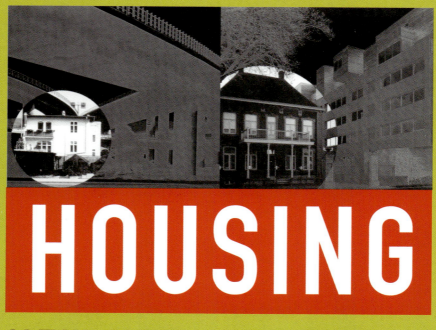

HOUSING

NEW URBAN SYSTEMS

II

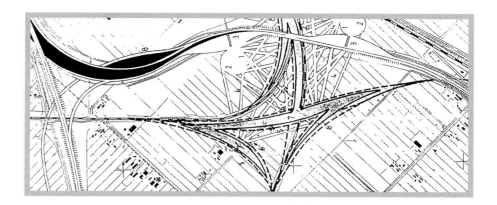

OMA. Interchangeable infrastructures and mechanisms. Transferium-Moordrecht 1992

1

HOUSING-CITY-TERRITORY

One of the major challenges of current critical thought on housing is, in effect, that of stimulating a renovation of residential space not only from the required spatial and technical reformulation of the given built 'cell', but also from the investigation of new urban orders.

▶ ORDERS CAPABLE OF BEING EFFECTIVELY RECONCILED WITH A NEW SETTING IN WHICH THE IDEA OF THE CITY AS A RECOGNIZABLE OUTLINE SET AGAINST AN 'EXTRA-MURAL' TERRITORY, AS A 'FIGURATIVE' LANDSCAPE CONFORMING TO PRECISE FORMAL DEFINITIONS, WOULD HAVE GIVEN WAY TO THE PRESENCE OF A NEW, MORE ALEATORY AND WILDER 'URBAN-TERRITORIAL' REALITY, articulated on different scales, no longer proceeding from the traditional continuity of the building process but from the strength and neutrality of the enormous networks intended to lend it support and of those differing autonomous events intended to guarantee its development.[25] Dynamics which would, in effect, have nothing to do with the autobiographical construction of the site (with the *genius loci* or gradual adaptation to the context) but which, more than to traditional criteria of implantation, would allude to strategic interests or factors involving external decision-making—of profitability and expansion —facilitated by the particular speed and efficiency, from a technological viewpoint, of new processes of planning and construction.

THE INFRASTRUCTURES OF COMMUNICATION AND TRANSPORT (MOTORWAYS, RAILROAD AXES, AIR TRAVEL CORRIDORS) APPEAR, IN EFFECT, AS THE MOST EVIDENT TRACES OF THIS COMPLEX TERRITORIAL SYSTEM.

Traces manifested as directive references for the future organization of the terrain: neutral nets independent of all building and marked by speed and sequentiality (and no longer by continuity and contemplation) and supportive of new 'commercial/service/leisure' activities, not just 'along' their lines but 'on' them, on various terrains first separated functionally and which today begin to absorb programs, complex and stratified in both

25. Cf. GAUSA, Manuel: "Systèmes ouverts vs. compositions fermeés," in the *Europan III* catalog, Europan, Paris, 1994

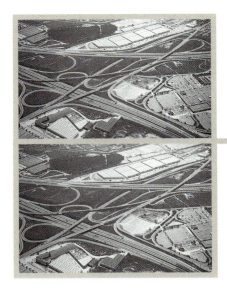

B

C

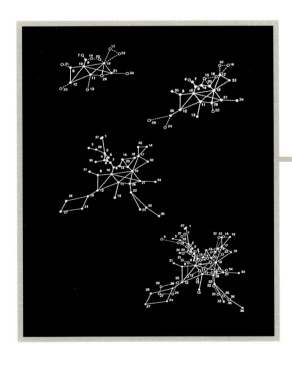

D

vertical and horizontal structures differing only in relation to the speed and means of locomotion. Fibrous networks—as **JOSEP LLUÍS MATEO** has appropriately defined them [26]—which transpierce syncopated developments, constructed archipelagos between those that are generated as emptiness; interstices, spaces at the edge or vast spaces of omission. Absences which function 'negatively'. Visual 'intervals' between arythmic events, destined to favor a new perceptual intelligence particularly sensitive to interruption and distortion, but also to intrusion, surprise and contrast. [27]

A SPACE, IN SHORT, IN WHICH EVEN THAT WHICH WE CALL 'PERIPHERY' COULD NO LONGER BE CONSIDERED A 'SITUATION' (THE CITY LIMIT ITS FRONTIER) BUT RATHER A 'CONDITION'

within the framework of a process—that of the dissolution of the urban in the territory—in which dispersed landscapes would coexist with relatively uncertain, even unfinished, margins and multifarious fragments defined by seemingly unrelated realities (historical nuclei, real estate operations, large-scale industry and warehouses, autonomous fixtures, areas of consumerism and leisure) mixed together with ephemeral presences (advertising slogans, technical structures, collectors and conductors of energy, temporary constructions) announcing that newly hybrid and progressively colonized state of the territory. [28]

A territory broken up by infrastructural signs which would tend to coexist with other connective networks—data programming, computing, finance; immaterial corridors out of which 'another' possible territory begins to establish itself, a global space de-territorialized by the instantaneity and immediacy of communication, and in which lack of 'access' would of necessity lead to marginalization, to another 'periphery' not necessarily situated now in the suburbs or urban limits but 'anywhere', thereby provoking profound changes in the traditional binomials 'residence/work' and 'city/territory'. [29]

The description of this new space of 'mobility' should not, however, be confused with the suggestion of one unique development:
if THE CONTEMPORARY 'METAPOLIS' IS NOT A PLACE OR A FORM, NEITHER IS IT A SINGLE EVOLUTIVE STATE, A SINGLE MOVEMENT, BUT INSTEAD THE ACCUMULATION OF MANY STATES: SIMULTANEOUS REALITIES, ACTIONS AND EXPERIENCES. A VIBRATORY, INCREASINGLY DIVERSIFIED SYSTEM PRODUCED BY ACCUMULATED, NON-FIXED REALITIES WHICH ARE CONTINUALLY PERVERTED AND TRANSFORMED.

A multi-scale territory which would manifest itself as a complex 'system' of relations and events determined by the successive layers of information and reference which make it up (physical but also demographic, biological, economic, cultural, political) and by the vast networks of articulation and interchange (of transport, energy, communication and diffusion, of financial movements, etc.) that structure it: layers and networks—whose data are not picked up in the specific place but generally from thousands of kilometers away, via satellite—and between which are produced simultaneous processes of action and reaction, combined according to their greater or lesser capacity for relation and modification, [30] thereby provoking movements of expansion and retraction in which 'locations are defined, regulations implemented, powers dissolved or strengthened and frontiers appear or disappear.' [31]

Ⓑ Barcelona-Vallès. Aerial views of the B-30. Photo: Manolo Laguillo

Ⓒ Network city. Courtesy Vicente Guallart-New Media (1995)

Ⓓ 1. Map of western Europe positing the connections between capitals. The black dots show spatial coordinates and their deformation, the white their respective temporal coordinates.
2. Flows of information in the control of airspace.

26. Cf. MATEO, Josep Lluís: 'Els immaterials,' in *Quaderns* 187, 1990.
27. Cf. GAUSA, Manuel: 'De la metròpolis a la metàpolis', op. cit.
28. 'In any completely urbanized space there will be little isolated pockets, reserves of agricultural land, national parks and business parks, tourist parks and residual parks intersected by transport networks, each one close to the next, without marginal space, without periphery'. Cf. STEINER, Dietmar: 'Vielleicht eine Biographie per Peripherie,' in *Daidalos* 50, 1993.
29. 'Individuals exist who will live in the real time of the world city, of the virtual community, and others who will live in postponed time, abandoned to the physical city, to its streets.' Cf. VIRILIO, Paul: 'Randgruppen,' in *Daidalos* 50, 1993.
30. Cf. GAUSA, Manuel: 'De la metròpolis a la metàpolis', op. cit.
31. Cf. DUPUY, Gabriel: *Systèmes, réseaux, territoires*, Presses Ponts et Chaussées, Paris, 1986.

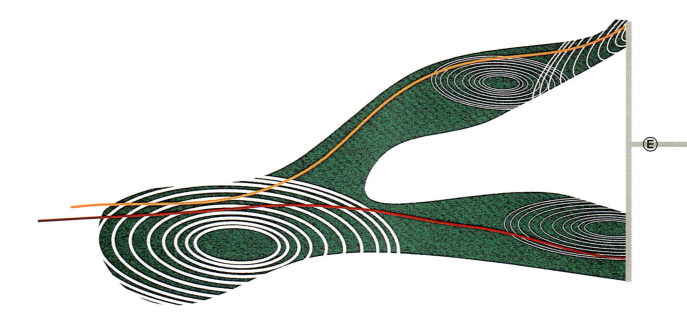

E

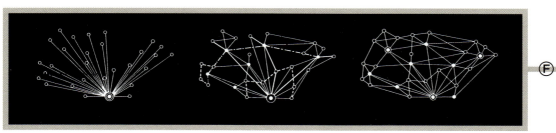

F

G

H

The contemporary 'metapolis' would constitute—as **FRANÇOIS ASHER** rightly says [32]—a new reality destined, from a variety of viewpoints, to supercede the city as we know it, and favoring a new type of urban conglomeration made up of vast heterogeneous and discontinuous urbanized spaces, produced by urban entities which are increasingly less identifiable with circumstances of spatial or contextual proximity but, on the contrary, with delocalized dynamics of a 'residence-production-service-leisure' variety.

LIKE A SPLATTERED INK STAIN, THE EXPANSION OF THE CONTEMPORARY METAPOLIS LEADS PROGRESSIVELY TO THE FORMATION OF MULTICENTRIC AND DISCONTINUOUS POLYNUCLEAR GROWTHS, BETWEEN WHICH APPEAR GAPS—HOLES, ABSENCES—AND SUB-PERIMETERS—LIMITS, EDGES—IN AN INCREASING PROCESS OF FRACTALITY provoked by a tendency (relatively recent from the viewpoint of urban anthropology) favoring, as in the well-known rug of Sierpinski, an irregular distribution of the total mass over the available surface area (distant, then, from the compact secular form) and thus multiplying such situations of proximity to a 'border' (privileged by their better access to the open spaces of the margin and to those networks of perimetral communication).[33]

THE INTEREST OF THAT PROCESS OF DISSOLUTION (THAT APPARENT AND ACCELERATED 'GASIFICATION' OF A FORMERLY SOLID BODY WHICH WOULD SUDDENLY LEAD TO ITS OWN VOLATIZATION) WOULD NOT LIE, THEN, SO MUCH IN THE EXACT VERIFICATION OF A MODEL, RECURRENT ON A GLOBAL AND MACROSCOPIC SCALE, AS IN THE MULTIFARIOUS SITUATIONS OF ACTION AND PERTURBATION, OF INTRUSION, INFILTRATION AND COMBINATION THAT CONSTANTLY PERVERT THE PURITY OF THE SCHEME, causing its abstract definition to mutate and transforming it into specific forms and configurations: fissures, collisions, encounters and intersections which ultimately engender perturbations and modifications within the process and endow each particular situation with a certain richness.

The city is no longer an 'island' but a nexus of many events—'cities within the city', as **DIRK HELBING** points out [34]—and, like any global nexus that develops under the direct influence of varied factors, it ends up being the non-planned, and not always foreseen, result of successive operations of planned intent: developments with their own factors of distortion which modify the anticipated changes and involve new movements in a progressively self-organized global structure assimilable to many others existing in nature (veins in an insect's wings, irrigation channels, fissures in the process of fracturing, air packaged as bubbles, etc.) in which relatively simple processes result in enormous levels of complexity; structures which, in spite of their diversity, adjust their shape to certain basic rules of spatio-temporal definition, analyzed by various areas of science and accessible to progressively abstract alternative models of analogy and simulation which are capable of representing, in a way that is more tactical than literal, that multifarious and interactive new system and its particular capacity for modification.[35]

Ⓔ Turbulences and nodes of growth in the new selective polycentric dynamics and urban growth

Ⓕ Three models of metropolitan structure: radial mononuclear, semireticulated multihierarchical and reticulated polynuclear

Ⓖ Superimpositions of strata. Multilayered city-vibratile city (*Väg-Och Vattenbyggaren*, 4/90)

Ⓗ Codifications. Abstract surveying structures and a 'figurative' translation of visualization strategies in a thematic map.

32. Cf. ASHER, François: *Métapoles ou l'avenir des villes*, Odile Jacob, Paris, 1995.
33. 34. Cf. HELBING, Dirk et al.: 'Strukturbildung dynamischer Systeme,' in *Arch + 121*, 1994.
35. Models of occupation according to the manner of 'acceding' to a superfice (minimal paths, direct paths) and the manner of proceeding to its appropriation (by systems analogous to the structure of bubbles, sand, etc.). Cf. BECKER, Sybille et al.: 'Selbstorganisation urbaner Strukturen,' in *Arch + 121*, 1994.

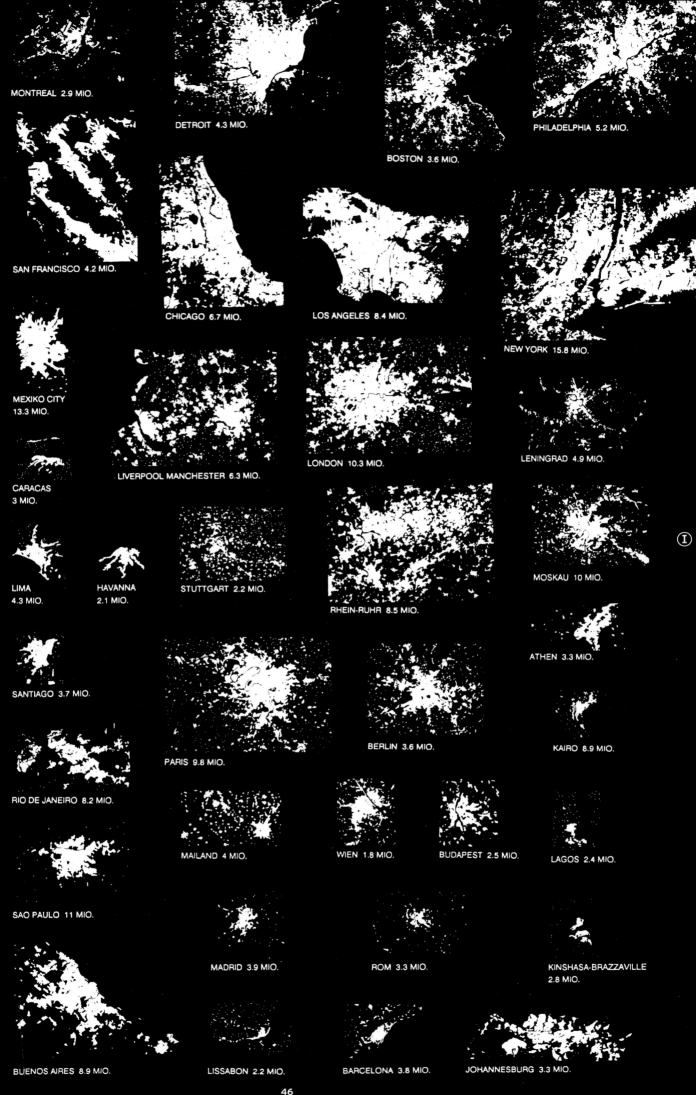

TO MAP THIS NEW REALITY BORN OF MOBILITY AND INTERCHANGE, OF MIGRATION AND COMMUNICATION, EFFECTIVELY REQUIRES RESOLUTE ATTENTION BEING PAID TO THOSE STRATEGIC FACTORS CAPABLE OF GENERATING POTENTIAL DEVELOPMENTS WITHIN THE SYSTEM:

superimpositions, ramifications, extensions, translations at a distance from the space being analyzed, a space marked by many variables but also by immaterial connections. More than a uniquely spatial structure the city is, then, a temporal process, a 'becoming', in which are involved both its formal components and, above all, its specific organizing structure and its capacity for interaction and synergy.[36] It is difficult, then, to try and embrace this whole fractal universe in transformation using the canonic instruments of a disciplinary criticism which is still reliant on a hypothetical coherence within its categories. In fact, if the dichotomy between a 'center' congealed by history and a still-expectant periphery constituted—in its time—a revitalizing *leitmotif* of recent urbanism, it was also going to end up limiting the debate to a kind of aesthetic confrontation between two figurative landscapes (that of recreated history and that of a potential dream of re-encountered modernity).

Each approach would desire a redemption of the urban, emerging from different codes yet both based on a totalizing design in the intervention, assimilating the urban project to a problem of 'planning', to, in the last analysis, the closed 'composition' of processes.

A desire for control that has characterized the particular limits of those models which the architectonic culture of the last twenty years has tried to use one after the other (the morphological continuity of the traditional city or the objectual freedom of modernity) and which would end in reducing understanding of the contemporary city and space to problems of figuration: old or new figurations undertaken, in any event, from a position of strict control of the processes.

Finite, closed products, complete in themselves.

① 'Ink stain' growth. The structures of the conurbations present certain similarities regardless of context. Global systems modified according to particular situations.
Topos, European Landscape Magazine, "Lanscape on the Urban Finge", 17, December 1996, Munich

36. Cf. KRAFT, Sabine: 'La Dynamique des villes,' in *Europan III*, op. cit.

A continent like a vast city. Europe from the point-of-view of energy consumption: map created from an abstractly-rendered satellite image (cf. *You Are Here*, MACBA, 1995).

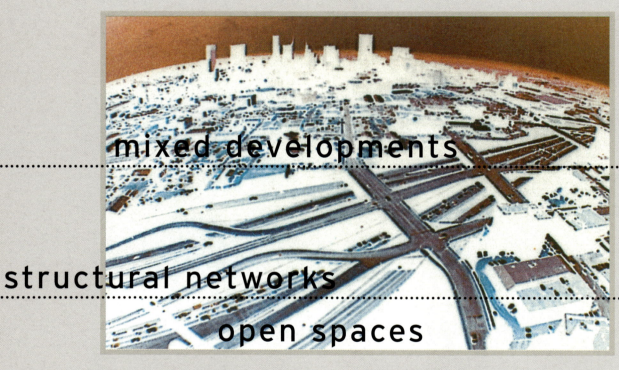

mixed developments

structural networks

open spaces

metropolitan radiography

2

OPEN SYSTEMS: POTENTIAL ENCODERS

The most interesting thing about this multi-scale space of cohabitation is precisely its problematic adscription within a unique theoretical or formal model. On the other hand, its understanding is possible merely from the accumulation and simultaneity of strata and movements, vibratory layers in civilized collision rather than in harmonious continuity;

ELEMENTAL STRUCTURAL PROCESSES OF A SURPRISINGLY GLOBAL CHARACTER, YET OPEN TO SUCCESSIVE, NOT NECESSARILY COHERENT, SINGLE EVENTS IN A DIFFUSE MINGLING OF THE GLOBAL AND THE PARTICULAR,

the systematic and the exceptional, the structured and the informal, the abstract and the concrete, as a hypostasis traduceable to the architectonic project, metaphor, in the final analysis, of the specific contemporary setting.

In that sense, the importance of the contribution of certain recent proposals is precisely their desire to develop a project dynamic–formal and structural methods–capable of synthesizing, with a greater or lesser degree of complicity, such phenomena; phenomena more strategic than figurative, more expressive than anecdotic, more related to lines of basic and immaterial force than to the specific design of the elements which today affect that future 'metapolitan space'.

METHODOLOGIES IN WHICH THE THEME OF HOUSING – THE CITY'S BASIC MATERIAL – WOULD GO BEYOND THE ROLE TRADITIONALLY LIMITING IT TO QUESTIONS OF FIGURATIVE OR TYPOLOGICAL DESIGN, AND ASSUME ANOTHER POTENTIAL STRUCTURAL FUNCTION RELATED MORE CLOSELY TO THE ARTICULATING SYSTEMS WHICH TODAY ORGANIZE CONTEMPORARY URBAN SPACE THAN TO THOSE TRADITIONAL AND LABORED COMPOSITIONAL YEARNINGS WHICH ARE LIMITED TO 'REFIGURING' IT.

reference
Mixed Developments

main idea
growth

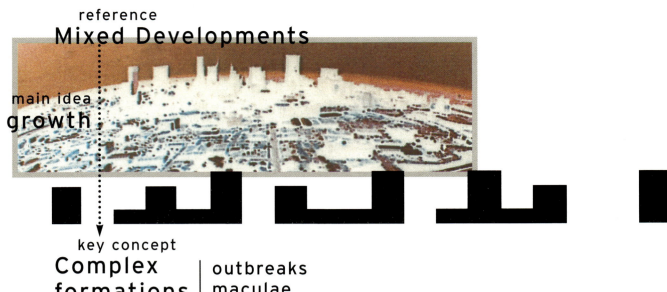

key concept
Complex formations | outbreaks maculae

reference
Structural networks

main idea
net

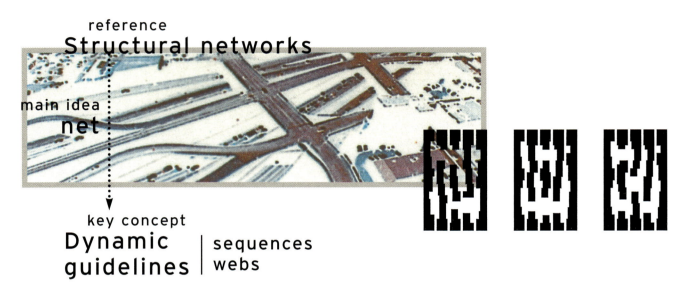

key concept
Dynamic guidelines | sequences webs

reference
Open spaces

key concept
landscape

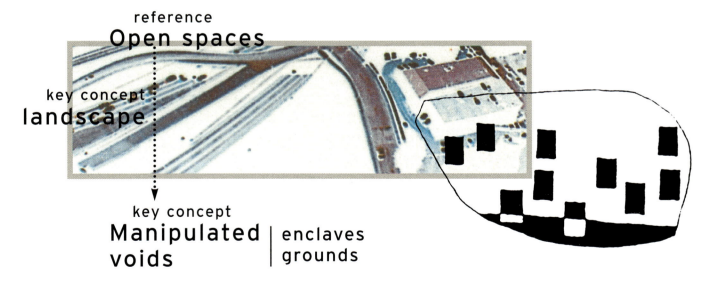

key concept
Manipulated voids | enclaves grounds

SYSTEMS which, far from being regenerative models (or intrusions) or ideal *tabulae rasae*, would seek to favor other, more versatile types of ORDER (drastic and respectful at the same time) in distant and also civilized cohabitation with the multiplicity of heterogeneous signs which characterize contemporary urban space.

◗ Orders generated by a tactical infiltration of reality rather than by the imposition of prefigured codes.

◗ Orders arising in direct response to solicitations and diagnoses that are at once programmatic and spatial; the positive responses of a new, atypological, open-form architecture disposed to accept the cohabitation of different stimuli as something of possible value, an 'anti-compositional' architecture which would end up orienting the project towards the idea of new articulatory systems.

◗ OPEN SYSTEMS with an important degree of abstraction in their conception, sensitive to the potential of variation, perturbation and distortion: to that constant interaction between strata which defines contemporary reality and which would take progressive variation and enrichment to be characteristics inherent to the processes themselves.

◗ Systems which, as has already been pointed out, would understand the form of the project more as a 'stand by', as a phase in the theoretical framework of a dynamic process: one potential combination among many latent combinations. [37]

◗ Systems capable of guaranteeing a particular accord with the site and, at the same time, of referring the project to a global dynamics, born of the specific reading and interpretation of that new 'metapolitan' identity: A SPACE OF STRUCTURAL NETWORKS, MIXED DEVELOPMENTS AND INTERSTITIAL OPEN SPACES AS SYNTHETIC REFERENTS OF THAT NEW DIMENSION OF THE CITY TO WHICH THE PROJECTURAL METHODOLOGIES HERE DESCRIBED WOULD IDENTIFY.

◗ Systems conceived as DYNAMIC GUIDELINES defined according to EVOLUTIVE TACTICAL SEQUENCES AND WEAVES, associated with the syncopated perception and with the matricial—arterial—configuration itself of vast STRUCTURAL NETWORKS.

◗ Or methodologies conceived on the basis of COMPLEX FORMATIONS as heterogeneous growths consisting of variable, juxtaposed OUTBREAKS and MACULAE, which would refer to the MIXED VOLUMETRIC DEVELOPMENTS of the huge archipelagos built on the territory.

◗ Or structures which are manifested as MANIPULATED VOIDS, both in their presence as support ENCLAVES—'FIELDS'—and in their manifestation as new operative GROUNDS (artificial topographies, reliefs) that would identify with the force of INTERSTITIAL OPEN SPACES.

(And lastly, following from this new instrumental knowledge and as a corollary to it, a gaze directed towards the consolidated FABRICS and their capacity for adopting restructuring interventions of TRIMMING AND DILATION).

A. Dynamic guidelines (sequences and webs)
B. Complex formations (outbreaks and maculae)
C. Manipulated voids (fields and grounds)

AS POSSIBLE ENCODERS OF THAT DESIRE FOR ACCORD BETWEEN THE NEW FORMAL DEVICES GENERATED AROUND THE CONTEMPORARY RESIDENTIAL PROJECT AND THE SPECIFIC MOVEMENTS OF THE CURRENT CITY: DEVICES—AND IDEOGRAMS—LESS AS LITERAL DESCRIPTIONS THAN AS CONCEPTUAL INSTRUMENTS INTENDED TO FAVOR A NEW, MORE OPEN CORRESPONDENCE BETWEEN FORM AND CONCEPT.

37. Cf. GAUSA, Manuel: 'De la metrópolis a la metápolis,' op. cit.

reference **Structural**
Networks

main idea **Net**

sequences

webs

key concept **Dynamic**
Guidelines

up: Dynamic perception: *Paris-Texas.* Wim Wenders, 1984
down: Infrastructures in Atlanta. Ramon Prat, 1995

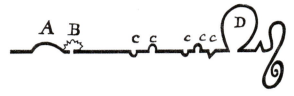 Ⓑ

 Ⓒ

 Ⓓ

Ⓔ

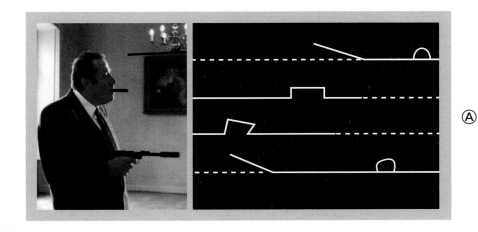

Ⓐ Pistol, cigar, guide. A sequence with variable elements.

A.1. SEQUENCES: series, cadences, counterpoints

Confidence in the sequential but not strictly repeated action—the serial succession—of referential elements would characterize those systems conceived more as abstract cadences intended to provide guidelines for space than as a strict orders intended to guarantee its continuity. Open sequences—more tactical than reiterative—as a spatial device associated with a new 'tempo'—that of mobility and displacement—and with the concomitant perceptive intelligence, in which the classic gaze (of gradual and harmonic narrative durations, and persistent and continuous familiar images) would have been substituted by a syncopated gaze made up of discrete perceptions: brief fragments, dynamic segments, fleeting presences, arhythmic events...

Ⓑ Laurence Stern. The novel as city (*Tristram Shandy*) in *New York-Normadesign*, Ed. b.b. 1992

Ⓒ Unpredictable situation in a 'predictable' landscape. *Vertigo*, Alfred Hitchcock, 1958

DIRECTIVE, FLAT IMAGES, LINES OF TENSION DISPOSED AS DISCONTINUOUS SERIES IN THE LANDSCAPE AND CONFIGURING A BASIC OPERATIVE ORDER

—more structural than compositional—capable of engendering basic rhythms and at the same time of absorbing dissociative elements: accidents, interruptions, local processes—counterpoints—alien to the system. Systems related *a priori* to many of the earliest experiments undertaken by modernity (conjunctions based on blocks, bars, points, etc.) and which should be interpreted as current reformulations of those pioneering devices reliant on the object's freedom over space. A concept whose exploration goes scarcely further than the elementariness and repetitive rigidity with which most of the early models were conceived, interventionary models still over-indebted to a totalizing and compositional vocation. The 'anonymous', abstract quality of that rhythmic potential particular to sequential seriality would today be combined, though, with a new interest in favoring movements and processes capable of subverting the adopted system itself: 'counter-rhythms' provoked by deformations and perturbations at the core of the adopted scheme itself or dissonances produced by 'intrusive' elements with their own autonomous configurations:

Ⓓ Kazuyo Sejima. Ideogram of movements for his zig-zag typologies. 'Metropolitan Housing Studio' (1995-96)

Ⓔ Lynne Cohen. Laboratory from *Occupied Territory*, Aperture Foundation, New York, 1987

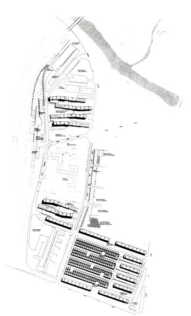

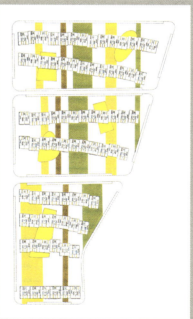
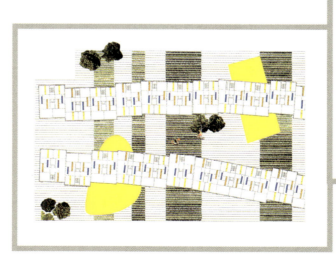

THE USE OF ELEMENTAL SCHEMES OF 'SERIATION' WOULD THUS PERMIT THE CONFIGURING OF A BASIC ORDER IN AN ONGOING SITUATION OF 'SUSPENSE' BETWEEN THE PREDICTABLE (THE REITERATED) AND THE UNFORESEEABLE (THE SINGULAR), DISTINCT FROM THE URGE TO CONTROL AND THE FORCED RIGIDITY IMPLICIT IN OTHER FORMULATIONS DEVELOPING OUT OF STRICT REPETITION,

open systems disposed to also admitting multifarious variations and perversions (distortions, sudden movements of the defined elements, intrusive presences, be they pre-existing or added) without ceasing, thereby, to favor effective 'directional tensions' in a 'guidelined' rather than prefigured landscape.

Systems which are also especially susceptible to the meaning of the 'temporary lapse'—in this instance spatial—between events, and hence in those where rhythmic 'silence'—the void, interstitial open space—would take on a particular importance, both in its disposition and its treatment.

O.M.A.'s emblematic project for the 'Y-Plein' sector of Amsterdam (1988) – a series of narrow bands constructed in precise dissonance—would stand, due to incorporation of brief tactical movements and added autonomous elements, as one of the earliest recent examples oriented towards re-examining the potential implicit in that diatony between 'predictability' (repetition) and distortion (surprise). The **'ZIG-ZAG** typologies' conceived by **KAZUYO SEJIMA** in his 'Metropolitan Housing Studio' (1995-1996)[38]–a series of rhythmic bars with small furuncules conceived as strange eruptions, ramifications of individual growth based on a host of spikes in motion—would constitute the most recent example of a form of action that would also take in projects like **SAUERBRUCH-HUTTON**'s for Berlin (1994), or the B.D.G. team's for Bilbao, and **GARCÍA DE PAREDES-PEDROSA**'s for Aranda de Duero (Europan IV, 1994), which also appears to be exploring that attempt at making strict sequential movements compatible with strategic acts of distortion, more in keeping with the specificity of each situation. The works of the **ACTAR ARQUITECTURA** team prosecute similar aims, both in their schemes for Son Gibert (Majorca, 1993) and Graz (1996), and in their project for Aubervilliers (Paris, 1996). A variable but never rigid or strictly equidistant series of longitudinal 'vibratory' sections (with internal movement and specific deformations) models the space, generating interrelated spatial vectors. These are entities conceived as 'synchronic mechanisms' designed to restructure, through their ambiguous seriality, a reality assimilable to a virtual battlefield in which the new directives would be 'lines of force' destined to accommodate elements of pre-existing reality, aleatory presences or 'infiltrated' events alien to the system but incorporated within it.

Mechanisms, in any event, based first and foremost in a constructional sequentiality open to the arhythmic and to surprise, and hence particularly sensitive to that fragile equilibrium between seriation and sudden shock, rhythm and distortion, control and chance which itself characterizes the dynamic perception of the contemporary landscape.

38. Cf. the monograph *Kazuyo Sejima*, El Croquis, Madrid, 1995.

Ⓕ 1 & 2: OMA. Y-Plein sector, Amsterdam 1988

Ⓖ 1, 2 & 3: B-D-G Studio. Housing project for the Mina de Morro (Europan IV). General plan and partial views.

Ⓗ 1, 2 & 3: García de Paredes-Pedrosa. Urban development in Aranda de Duero (Europan IV, 1996). General plan, partial plan and detail of built sequences.

Ⓘ Actar Arquitectura. 300 housing units in Son Gibert (Majorca 1993). General plan and partial plan. The act of building as a vibratile guideline.

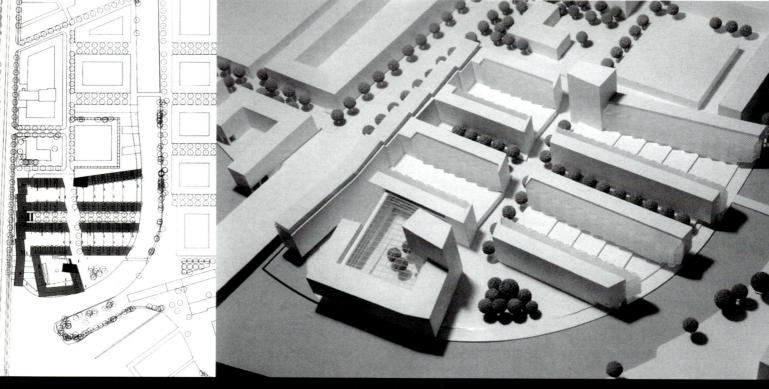

MATHIAS SAUERBRUCH
LOUISA HUTTON

Maselakekanal

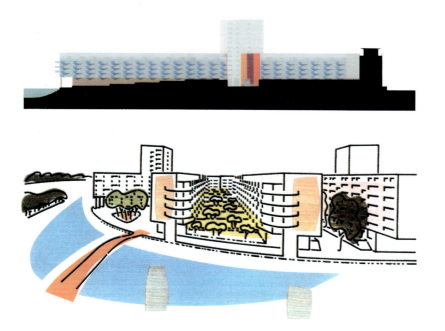

MASTER PLAN FOR A
RESIDENTIAL QUARTER

Situated right beside the river, the project was intended to provide maximum contact with the water, something impossible to achieve in a traditional scheme of city blocks and streets.
The proposal 'opens up' the original structure, while maintaining its density. Allowing for the sun and trying to reduce noise pollution from the main street and an adjacent factory, the area is divided into spaces facing the street, and others the interior gardens.
The parking areas under the gardens create a change of level and a proportional difference between the lowest garden section and the highest part of the street.

JOSÉ GONZÁLEZ GALLEGOS
M. JOSÉ ARANGUREN

Towers of Light

The planned volumes are configured as an alignment of vertical prisms, with multiple grooves or incisions—the gallery-window edges—which, when seen at night, would appear as 'Towers of Light'. Faced with the diversity of the surrounding buildings, the scheme responds with the device of a musical repetition which articulates a number of urban spaces opening onto the city, spaces that are ample, due to the fact of building upwards.

The ordered movement of the compositional elements above the block gives rise to interesting spatial relationships in which the perspectives spanning the whole site in its main directions open and close. The housing units, the greater part of the project, are constructed using a system of mean heights which gives the possibility of dominating the maximum dimensions of the dwelling, of segregating without cutting and, simultaneously, of affording the possibility of the hierarchization of public to private space without partition walls. This three-dimensional character adds a quality that transcends housing as something laminated or stratified, lacking in spatial intensity.

Views of the model

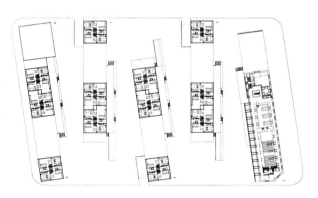

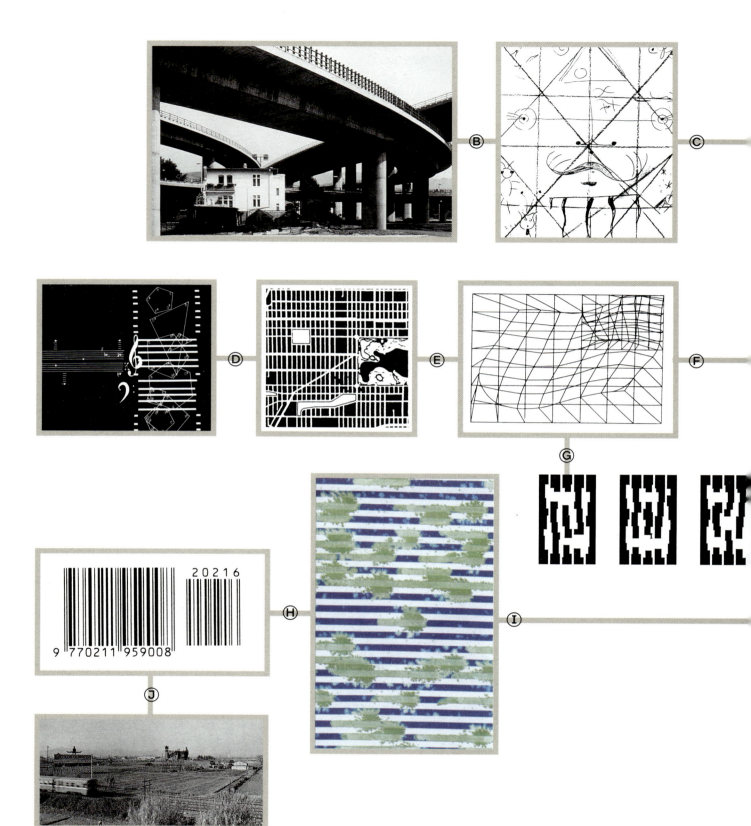

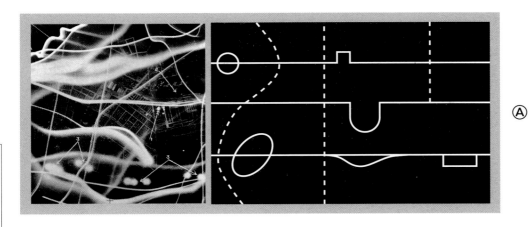

ⓐ 'Royal Air Force': Night Raid over Berlin, 1993 (cf *Urban Visions*, CCCB-Electra, 1994)

A.2. WEBS: nets, rails, circuits

The emphasis on the definition of a supporting flexible web characterizes those schemes most attentive to the conception of 'evolutive matrices', guidelines that are simple in essence but capable of generating varied and complex configurations out of the optimization, and at the same time distortion, of their given elemental definition.

Weaves which would refer to the abstract definition itself of vast infrastructural networks of territorial articulation: elemental regular forms, 'traces' more than 'tracings' of reference and structuration.

Weaves like those defined BY REFERENTIAL NETS ('grilles', 'gratings') of recognizable and/or deformed geometries, but with the capacity of overcoming the rigid reticular order and favoring flexible nets: combinatory 'checkerboards'. OR MATRICES THOUGHT OF AS ELEMENTARY BAR CODES, systems of bands made up of parallel, contiguous and interlaced RAILS (webs, then, more than rhythms) which would be conceived of less as strictly zonificatory geometries than as more or less dilated 'furrows of movement'.

The paradigmatic O.M.A. project for Fukuoka (1993)—a dense tapestry consisting of three functional bands alternating with three service fascia (with their respective transversal subdivisions) as the basis for a reticle which is seemingly rigid, yet manifested externally as a fluid form, thanks to the dynamic movement of the section and the strategic cutting of the perimetral edges—would refer to that idea of a flexible framework implicit in the first hypothesis. In turn the 'low-altitude typology' conceived by KAZUYO SEJIMA for his already-mentioned 'Metropolitan Housing Studio'[39]—a net basically made up of nine parallel bands within which residential units alternate with private gardens, precisely curtailed by the aleatory outline of an interior street and a circular related space—or the project by ADRIAAN GEUZE & WEST 8 for the Borneo Sporenburg area (Amsterdam, 1993-96)—a structure designed from five large parallel strips which accommodate in their interior an unending succession of tablet-like constructions, a 'sea' of residential units in which are housed three large intrusive blocks that break the sequence of repetition and refer the complex to other scales—appear to respond, rather, to systems conceived from the definition of parallel 'rails'. Systems which,

ⓑ Knot. Reinhardt Patz. 1981

ⓒ Joan Miró. Preparatory study. A basic grid and autonomous presences

ⓓ John Cage. Score

ⓔ Manhattan. Regular web and perturbations to it

ⓕ Peter Eisenman. Deformed web for Rebstock Park, Frankfurt (1991)

ⓖ Faro Architekten. Ideogram of web patterns for Emmen (1996)

ⓗ Bar code (*Quaderns*)

ⓘ Bruno Munari. Textile design. Regular code and irregular spots (in *Far vedere l'aria*, Lars Müller, Zürich, 1995)

ⓙ Rails and movement Photo: John Davies Llobregat, 1990

39. Cf. the monograph *Kazuyo Sejima*, El Croquis, Madrid, 1995.

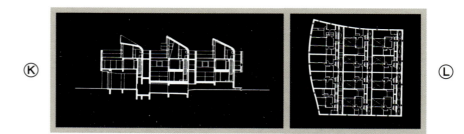
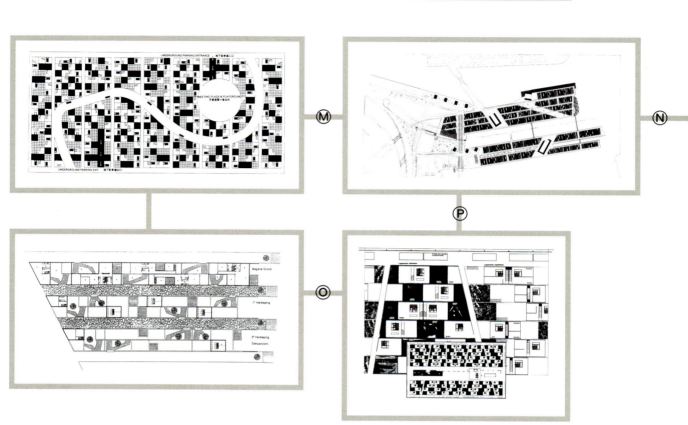
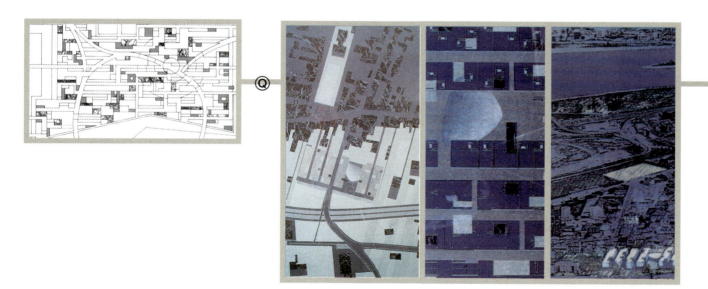

through their very configuration, at once flexible and rigid, would permit organizing, via successive movements of displacement and slippage in the various subdivisions, the particular inhabited cell and the processes of growth to which the latter is referred, alternating empty and full, private and public fields, and so combining many situations simply by the differing disposition of sliding elements (transverse walls, patios, service cores, interior and exterior spaces), of the incisions produced (cuts, rips, inflections) and also of the chance appearance of elements independent of the proposed system itself (absorbed volumes or incorporated autonomous forms).
The proposals put forward by ROAGNA EHRENSPERGER-CELLINI for Yverdon or by DE CLERQ-VAN DER PLOEG-WEIJNEN-WILLEMEN for S-Hertogenbosch (Europan III, 1992) deal with some of those possibilities by adopting certain modular schemes with a differing potential for variation. The proposal of ROAGNA-EHRENSPERGER-CELLINI has a strong conceptual basis in being created as an articulating carpet of movements which are 'deposited' on an open-plan structural base, designed for being colonized by businesses, offices, parking lots, etc.
On this immaterial socle there evolves, on two non-homogeneous levels, a story of apartments and workshops of differing size, proceeding from the disposition of the variable positioning of a series of parallel rails in which the inhabitable spaces are defined by the variable positioning—on the stagger—of the transverse divisions, thus creating a basic rhythm of open and occupied spaces with eventual increases in height.
The proposal of DE CLERQ-VAN DER PLOEG-WEIJNEN-WILLEMEN also appears to be moving in this direction. Here too the disposition in parallel bands perpendicular to the artery of communication permits the linking up of the site, proceeding from a scheme accordable with other situations. Longitudinal rails which support various internal subdivisions give way alternately, via a number of transversal and longitudinal sliding movements, to the emergence of inhabitable and vacant surface areas with garden. Movements which are also produced in height via the variable emergence—in size and in time—of vertical excrescences, individual bodies in which auxiliary rooms are situated and which ultimately define a dynamic, quasi-aleatory outbreak on a continuous socle.
The proposals of REICHARDT-FERREUX for Pierre Bénite-Lyon (Europan III, 1992) and MVRDV for Delft (1996) are configured, rather, as 'circuits' inserted into the fabric: matrices of variable and open configuration.
The works of LACOSTE-ROBAIN for Dunkerque (Europan II, 1990) are also created from reticular frameworks thought of as basic matrices, but above all as 'landscapes' defined through the strategic treatment of the roofs, conceived as new artificial public surfaces, great voids of mineral appearance consistently understood from the variation and movement of the access elements.
Variations and movements, in any case, which would not be limited solely to the different horizontal positioning of two basic directives, orthogonal in reference, but which could also be produced in a freer way, by means of intrusions and extrusions, straight lines and curves, invading spaces, defining zones, superposing distinct levels, as in the interesting proposal of BEN VAN BERKEL for Borneo Sporenburg (Amsterdam, 1994), a dense network of small housing blocks organized in varied fashion through the superposition of 'irregular' layers, referred to an elementary structural norm based on four bays—which, in the last analysis, engender developments open to multiple and not always determined formal combinations, on an elementary referential matrix ALWAYS UNDERSTOOD AS A NEUTRAL WEB—AN INVISIBLE NETWORK—WHICH, HERE TOO, STRUCTURES EVENTS OF ITSELF.

Ⓚ OMA. Fukuoka Housing in form of a grille (1993)

Ⓛ Kazuyo Sejima. Low-level typology. Weave of bands and distortion-free elements

Ⓜ Adriaan Geuze & West 8. Master plan for Borneo Sporenburg (Amsterdam 1993-96). Rails of sequential development and intrusive elements at another scale.

Ⓝ De Clerk-Van der Ploerg-Weijnen-Willemen (S-Hertogenbosch. Europan III, 1992). Parallel borders of sequential colonization

Ⓞ Roagna-Ehrensperger-Cellini (Yverdon. Europan III, 1992). Parallel bands of sequential colonization

Ⓟ MVRDV. Delft 1996 Weave. Fabric as 'circuit of connections'. Matrix of open configuration

Ⓠ Reichardt-Ferreux (Pierre Bénite, Lyon. Europan III, 1992). Weave. Fabric as inserted circuit

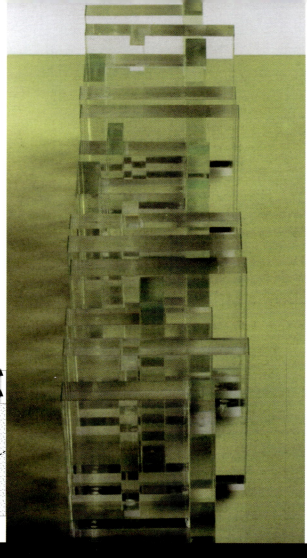

KAZUYO SEJIMA & ASSOCIATES

Housing Studies

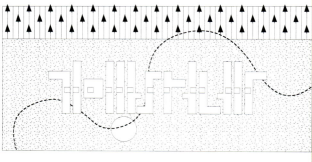

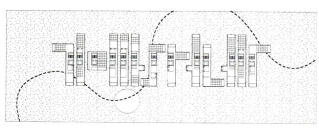

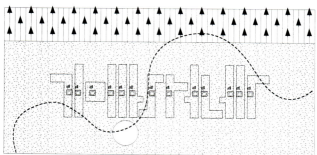

A TYPOLOGY OF HEIGHT DIFFERENCE: 10-STORY RESIDENTIAL MINIBLOCKS WITH CENTRAL CORE

A chain of blocks of highly unusual proportions, with one dwelling unit per floor, are located in the center of the site, with a large amount of open space around them. The restricted space between the blocks is intended as a visual, physical and psychological buffer zone for these high-rise towers.

12% occupation
Occupied surface: 1,236 m²
Built surface:
- 8,470 m² (housing)
- 1,518 m² (communal areas)
- 1,236 m² (pilotis)
Number of housing units: 117

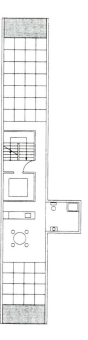

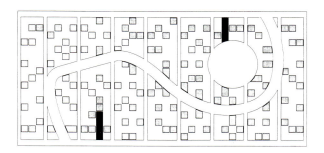

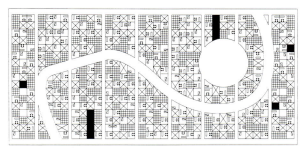

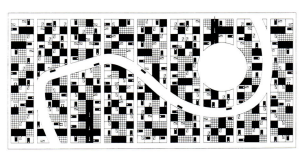

LOW-RISE TYPOLOGY WITH SEPARATE GARDENS
**(1-story underground parking +2-story units). The design is comprised of two-story units in maisonnete form.
Each unit is composed of six elements: open garden, kitchen-diner, utility space and three bedrooms. It also has a private garden on the roof as well as at ground level.**

Occupied surface: 6,034 m²
Built surface:
- 8,796 m² (housing)
- 3,240 m² (parking areas)
Number of housing units: 120

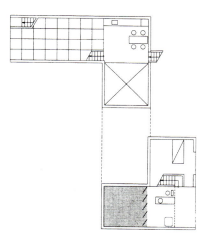

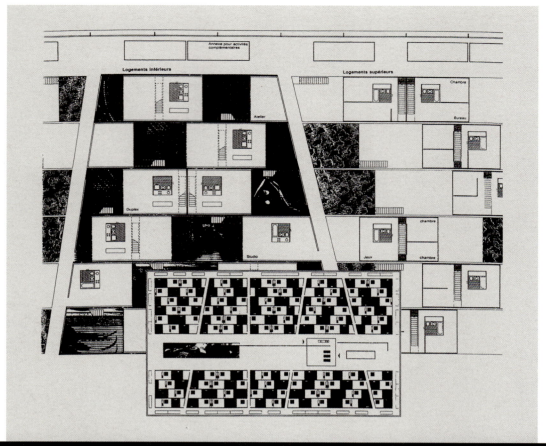

THIERRY ROAGNA
HANNES EHRENSPERGER
MARCO CENNINI

Compact urban block

The project proposes a compact, solid block covering the whole surface of the site, a "town within the town". The ground level is designed to accommodate mixed-use (leisure, small firms and warehouses), as well as other services and offices located on a mezzanine floor.
The first floor serves as a car park, while on the second floor there is access to the two levels of housing, arranged in bands alternating building and garden. On the access level there is a common area with swimming pool.

Yverdon. Europan 3, 1993.
Honourable mention

Compact urban block
Partial plan (lower and upper dwelling units) and general layout. Perspective view, structural principle and disposition of the various levels.

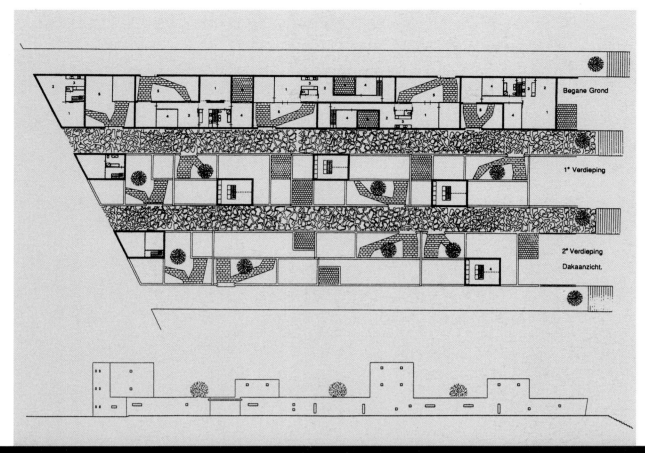

HUGO DE CLERCQ
JURGEN VAN DER PLOEG
PIETER WEIJNEN
ATALJA WILLEMEN

Series of experiences

The project proposes a linear structure comparable to a rake and a triangular complex of quiet streets which subdivides the public space in order to create an alternating structure of experiences and images.
The habitat is introverted, the public space turned towards the water. The linear construction in the form of a rake consists of linking buildings which resemble bayonets, while the triangular complex forms a spatial domino comprising four housing types: with patios, linked in a system of parallel bands, introverted, and with variable extensions and views over the water.

'S-Hertogenbosch. Europan 3, 1993.
Honourable mention

Triangular complex.
Floor plants, elevation and model.

THIERRY LACOSTE
ANTOINETTE ROBAIN

A dialogue between two territories

Windows on the sky. "It is not wishful thinking to want to order the future evolution of a city through and intervention on an enclosed plot of land, on the outskirts of the existing urban fabric, without access to the sea, or a direct view of the port." The project engages two territories: the harbor—an exploration of the void, punctuated with high buildings, a museum of mechanical cranes, a water garden—and the town—a low and compact habitat occupying the whole of the proposed site, a mass constructed like a piece of jigsaw puzzle in the urban fabric. The project questions the evolution of the town as a singular whole, working on the present contrasts rather than invoking a general homogenization. It nevertheless treats the housing as a single monolith and agglomerate of countless pieces.

Dunkerque. Winner. Europan 2, 1991

1

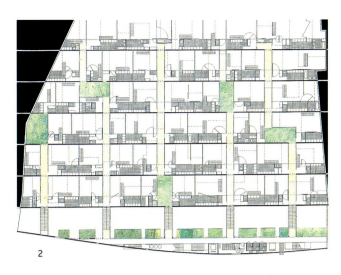

2

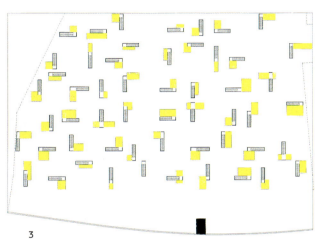

3

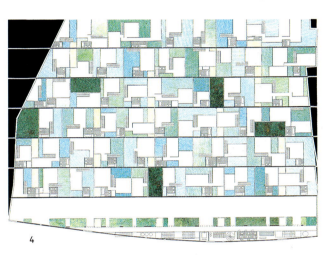

4

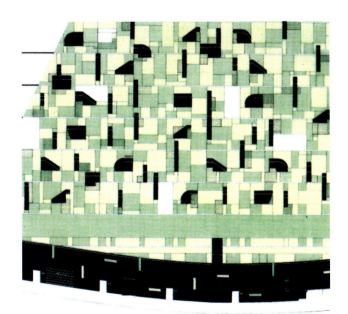

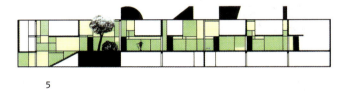

5

Plans
1. Level 0.0 Parking
2. Level + 2.5 Apartments
3. Level + 5.00 Apartments
4. Level + 7.50 Terrace
5. Transverse section

reference **Mixed developments**

main idea **Growth**

outbreaks

maculae

key concept **Complex Formations**

top: 'Profiles', Atlanta. Photo: Jordi Bernadó. *Atlanta* Ed. Actar. Barcelona, 1995
bottom: "Superposition" Beijing. Photo: Anna Puyuelo Barcelona, 1995

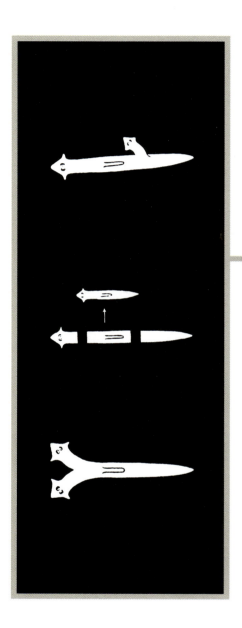

Ⓐ Dwarf and giant. Coexistence of scales (archive photo)

B.1. OUTBREAKS: profiles, excrescences, inflexions

The exploration of constructional orders evolving height-wise in free form, via the strategic use of the vertical dimension, would configure other system types related to the volumetric fractality itself of contemporary space: with that constant sensation of ambiguity of scale which characterizes a context consisting of successive developments rather than the purity of the already-built. A space open to formal mutation, to the intermixing of uses, to geometric complexity.

THE DEVICES DESCRIBED HERE WOULD BE CONFIGURED AS ARTICULATORY GROWTHS AND MOVEMENTS;

dynamic profiles on much lower bases; outbreaks, abscesses and egresses, vertical in impulse, silhouetted against the horizon; complex sections made up of independent strata and varied heights capable of favoring processes of growth adjusted to movements of event and outline; swerves and inflections between the full and the empty—between the built and the non-built—produced through the combination, at differing heights, of programs which are no longer rigidly separated but intermingled in mixed organisms of complex coexistence. 'Embedded' and jagged profiles in which the combination of spaces of variable density (horizontal expansions and vertical elevations, for example) would tend to favor a particular spatial vibration.

As **EDUARD BRU AND ENRIC SERRA** rightly point out,[40] this would have to do with a new concern for verticality, rather than a fascination with the skyline, growing out of the evidence of a new potential of scale and morphology implicated in the assumption of 'a three-dimensional dimension suited to superceding that historical city which, up to the beginning of the twentieth century, constituted a markedly two-dimensional space.'

Ⓑ Outbreaks and abscesses (in Greg Lynn: 'Multiplizitäre und unorganische Körper', Arch+, 119/120, 1993)

40. Cf. BRU, Eduard & SERRA, Enric: "Traspao de escala," in Quaderns 211, 1995

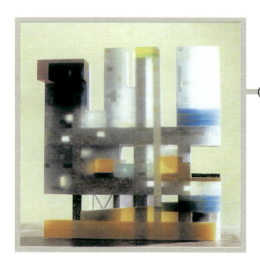

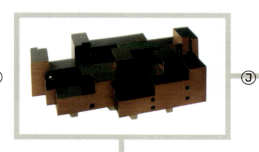
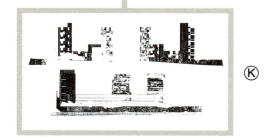

The well-known project of **HANS KOLLHOFF** for the 'H/C' Competition for the Diagonal in Barcelona (1990) would be a prime example of this kind of approach: the filling-up of the 'Cerdà' block, here understood as a process of repetition proper to the homogeneous city, consists of a continuous base from which materializations of a certain height would rise strategically: towers of varied height intended to dot the space in an aleatory manner, so creating a dispersed and dynamic new order on a neutral and stable socle.

The proposal of **EDUARD BRU & SERRA-CARTAGENA-VIVES** for Barcelona's Poble Nou seafront project (1995) goes further, and in greater detail, in this direction. The exceptional situation of the site, facing the vast emptiness of the sea, gives rise to a drastic change of scale in the city and a reflection on the 'Cerdà' connection itself, establishing a strategy of double-sequence by means of elements of alignment and elements developed height-wise. The ensemble calls on freedom of growth for its resolution: 'a constructed mass which empties itself or grows where it may, according to the simultaneous requirements of the historical and the living city. It is not a question, then, of establishing a structure of repetition but rather of an abstract system of rhythms and sequences open to varied and specific solutions.'[41]

Similar anxieties inform the projects of **MVRDV (MAAS-DE VRIES-VAN RIJS)** for Berlin (1990) and **DUWENSEE-KREPLIN** for Rostock (1990): urban megaforms which nevertheless adjust their profiles to the successive vicissitudes of the program and the intersection of tensions of the site itself: a hinged space between characteristic and discontinuous fabrics which favor processes of excision and fractality in the outline.

Faced with the conjoint variety of height and volume peculiar to the surroundings, the schemes of **ELLEN MONJEN AND AGNES BURG** for Münster (European III, 1994), or those of **ARANGUREN-GALLEGOS** for Cartagena and **LUIS MARTÍNEZ SANTA MARÍA** for Palma de Mallorca (Europan IV, 1996), or **AMANN-CÁNOVAS-MARURI** for Coslada (Madrid, 1996), also propose a strategic diversity resulting from variations that give rise to the vertical growths and excisions produced by constructed materializations based on repetition. Here, too, this gives way to dynamic growths, but above all to a possible cohabitation between different types and densities.

IN ANY EVENT, IT IS ALWAYS A QUESTION OF DEVELOPMENTS BASED ON THE FRAGMENTED AND VERTICAL DEFINITION OF THE FORM ITSELF,

no longer definable solely from the planned outline or volumetric regularity, but instead from that vocation for three-dimensional discontinuity, which would favor the combination of diverse developments or interventions in a single organism: developments favored, even, by different actors in particular syntony with each other.

SCHEMES, AT ALL EVENTS, WHICH WOULD COMPENSATE FOR VERTICAL CONCENTRATIONS WITH SUPERFICIES OF LESSER HEIGHT, LOW-DENSITY UNITS WITH UPWARD MOVEMENT, PURE VOLUMES OF 'RHIZOMIC' GROWTH WHICH ULTIMATELY FAVOR THE COEXISTENCE OF DIFFERING SCALES THROUGH THE VARIATION, JUXTAPOSITION AND ARTICULATION OF THEIR OWN PROJECTED PLAY OF VOLUMES.

© Dynamic outbreaks: Hans Kollhoff. Entry for the 'H/C' Competition (Barcelona 1990)

Ⓓ Mixed profiles: Bru & Serra-Cartagena-Vives. Project for the Poble Nou seafront (Barcelona 1995)

Ⓔ Emergences: Duwensee-Kreplin (Rostock 1990)

Ⓕ MVRDV. Urban megaform Europan, 1991

Ⓖ Gauged resections: Lacoste-Robain (60 housing units in Épinay-sur-Seine 1993)

Ⓗ Kees Christiaanse: housing block in The Hague, Kavel 25, 1989-92

Ⓘ Growths: Amann-Cánovas-Maruri: Housing units in Coslada (Madrid, 1996)

Ⓙ Dynamic profiles: Fernando Porras. Multiple organism 1995

Ⓚ Mixed profiles: Luís Martínez, Santa Clara (Mallorca–Europan IV, 1996)

41. Cf. the project statement.

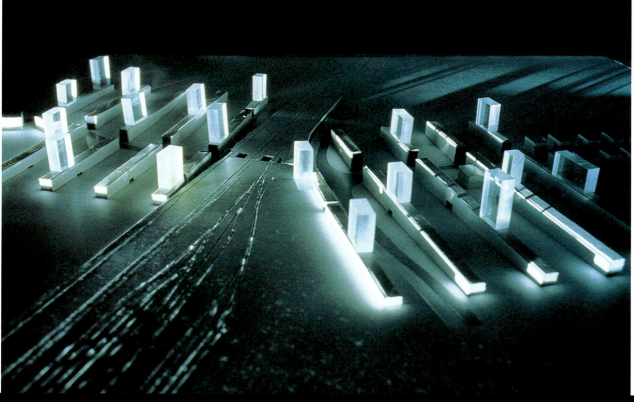

General views. Upper and lower levels

ELLEN MONJEN
AGNES BURG

Best of both worlds

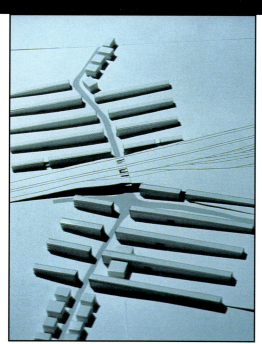

Between Ruhrgebiet
and Münsterland, this location
seems to be a battlefield of
conflicting entities: nature and
industry; road and railway;
community and outside world.
A stabilizing intervention is
required to establish a new
balance, transforming the loose
entities into the identifying
elements of a new configuration.
Two levels, two means
of transport, two forms of
perception.
By introducing bands of
"mixed functions" at ground
level, a sequence of scales is
created which links the
functions of daily life.
The trace of the Bahnhofstrasse
cuts through these bands.
The perception responds to a
rhythm of "mass/open space"
which contrasts with the
monotony of the usual ribbon
building. At upper level
there are no gradual sequences,
but rather abrupt confrontation
between interregional
railway travel and neighbourhood
intimacy. An abstract world of
roofs and tree tops. Here,
penthouse apartments stand as
solitary objects in the infinite
space which dissolves
all barriers and divisions.

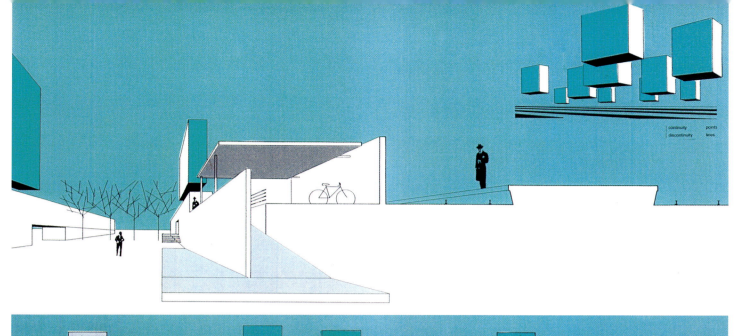

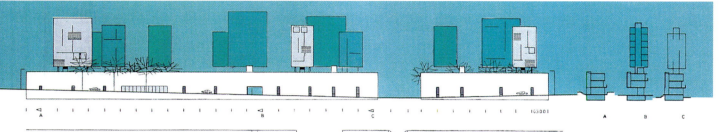

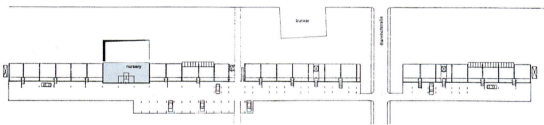

Section. The band of the station acts as a transitional element between the two levels. The roof of the lower level bands is the base for the penthouses. These have a neutral glass skin through which may be perceived the individual lifestyles of the occupants. Family housing units on the lower level. Common space and individual rooms shown in different configurations.

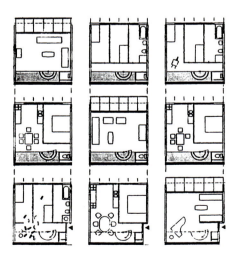

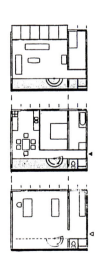

Penthouses on the upper level. "He loves his freedom. The interior of his apartment changes every two months, according to the latest fashion. The service core is the only stable factor of his life."

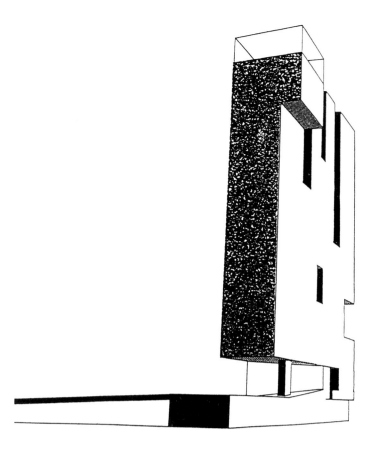

MVRDV — **Urban megaform**

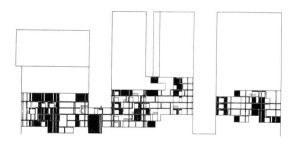

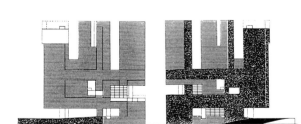

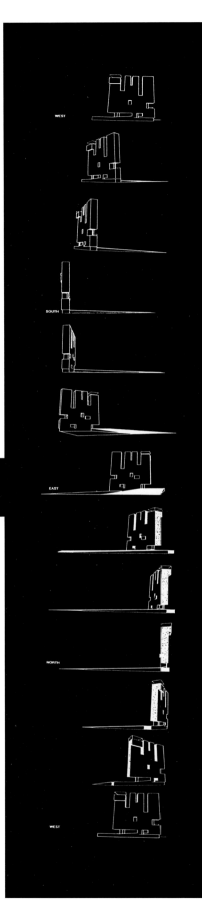

The project is posited as a meditation on 'dilation and 'concentration'. A definition of place is achieved by a vertical abstraction, an economy of means and a poetic use of voids. The 'slice' is a large multifunctional building of optimal height for 280 dwellings, which grows and is trimmed back as per the requirements of the program.

Elevations, sections and dynamic views of the building

N. de Vries, J. van Rijs, W. Maas: urban megaform for Berlin, Europan winner 1991

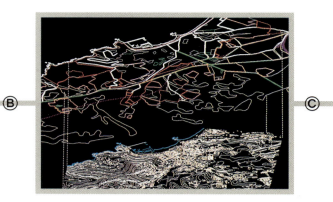

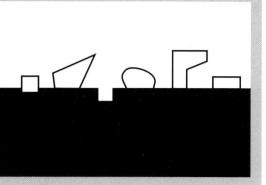

Commensalism and parasitism
Ⓐ Rhinoceros and bird.
In *Zoo Animals*,
Warne, London 1972

B. 2. MACULAE: grafts, parasitisms, commensalisms

In certain structures the idea of 'growth' finds itself exacerbated by the 'unnatural' contract, in a single project, of laws of diverse, at times contradictory, formation: 'maculae' evocative of a city formed of many stages, 'strata' generated in no longer homogeneous developments but intermixed, open to the ongoing coexistence of superposed autonomous elements intended to favor their own powerful dynamics of transformation. **MACULAE WHICH WOULD ALLUDE TO THE PROGRESSIVE DISJOINING OF THE PARTS OF THE CONTEMPORARY PROJECT.** but also to the interpretation of a city which is itself only representable today through the superposition of differentiated layers of information (as occurs in readings by scanner or in GIS infographic maps) with interconnected, but not necessarily symbiotic, data.

In fact, the strategy of combination and interrelation between autonomous organisms ('layers' of varied information) would allude to the urban form itself and its disintegration, as a harmonious and coherent entity, into a new 'simultaneous' landscape open to the union of disparate 'messages': maculae or grafts between foreign bodies which would appear as

SUPERPOSED OR JUXTAPOSED STRUCTURES PROCEEDING FROM FORMS DEVELOPED IN A COMMENSALIST MANNER ON OTHERS WHICH WOULD, IN TURN, PLAY THE PART OF 'HOST'

(as in the animal kingdom where certain parasitical species customarily bind themselves to others capable of sustaining their needs).

A vocationally 'hybrid' character–as **ALEJANDRO ZAERA** suggests, referring to the work of **STEVEN HOLL**[42]–would comply with the wish to explore effective 'anti-types' for a city ultimately lacking in formal typification. Anti-types which would nevertheless respond, not so much to programmatic admixtures as to localized stimuli related to the intersection of forces–perceptual, morphological, etc.–specific to places subject to simultaneous reference (the limits of the city, boundary spaces, etc.) and the shock between multifarious structures.

Ⓑ Juxtaposition, *Atlanta*
Photo: Ramon Prat

Ⓒ GIS. Analytical map
The city as
superimposition of layers

Ⓓ Juxtapositions, *Atlanta*
Photo: Ramon Prat

Ⓔ Hybridism: the grafting of objects to generate other products ('Flight-Fancy', in *I-D*, March-April 1994)

Ⓕ Antitypes and the disconnecting of parts.
Kas Oosterhuis.
Programmatic researches 1993

Ⓖ Roland Fässer.
Mutations (1992-95)

42. Cf. ZAERA, Alejandro: 'Steven Holl, hacia una estética de la reaparición,' in *Quaderns* 197, 1993.

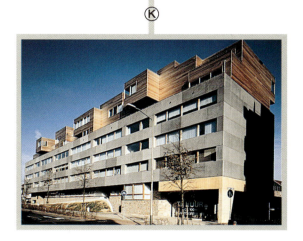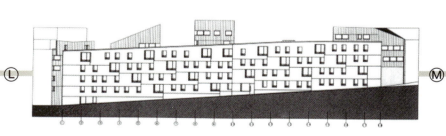

Some of these considerations are tested programmatically in **STEVEN HOLL**'s project for Makuhari (1994-96). A marginal site on the edge of Tokyo Bay is home to a scheme formed by the juxtaposition of two differing and opposed structures based on heavy, slightly distorted built masses (destined to receive the greater part of the collective residential program) and small individual elements, strange infiltrating presences in miniature, foreign to the general system (suited to favoring more individualized personal programs): 'individual sounds on a soundless mass.'

This dual coexistence is, if possible, even more evident in the project of **EDUARD BRU AND OAS** for Cerdanyola (Barcelona, 1994); the opposition between structural and morphological systems produced by the implicated territory (between the vast infrastructures which might pass through it and the dispersed, almost clandestine urbanizations that punctuate it) is traduced in the project by means of a 'direct macula between two types of built forms', shaped respectively by a neutral base, four floors in height (having the same conceptual quality as a viaduct) and a series of small individual volumes colonizing its roof and which relate to the many independent particles that characterize the neighbouring occupational structures.

The Prinsenhoek building of **WILLEM JAN NEUTELINGS** (Sittard, 1992-95) is also defined in similar terms as a hybrid structure capable of acting powerfully on an urban scale, while at the same time responding to the varied solicitations of the site. Like some vast infrastructure, a large neutral base accommodates a serial succession of individual units lodged guest-like on the roof and conceived as a translation in height of the domestic scale particular to the immediate surroundings.

In the 'multi-cantilever' building projected by **MVRDV (MAAS-VAN RIJS-DE VRIES**, Amsterdam 1996) **THIS PRESENCE OF AUTONOMOUS ORGANISMS WHICH ARE 'PARASITICAL'** on an organism of superior size is also radically manifested in both the expressive treatment of the many individual elements (balconies, windows, etc.) which colonize the facade and the huge cantilevered eruptions which flank the building; excrescences flying off from a basic referential volume.

The theoretical works of **KAS OOSTERHUIS** and his built works in Groningen (1995-96), as well as the proposals of **WILLEM JAN NEUTELINGS** for Ghent (1996-97) and Borneo Sporenburg (1995), or the project by **LACOSTE-ROBAIN** for Partants (Paris, 1992), enable them to go further along this road towards a potential mutation based more on mixed cohabitation—and on parasitical commensalism—than on harmonious coexistence; the combination of strata of varied formalization (some more repetitive and general, other less predictable and individual) is manifested in methodologies usually generated by, on the one hand, prismatic, predictable and neutral basic structures, and on the other, by enjambed elements, individualized to the maximum: intrusive structures that are formally variable and indeterminate. While 'normal' apartments, standard spaces, are generally accommodated in that first neutral socle, providing a first and basic level of reading, the free development of the individual units (duplex, triplex, studios, etc.) would conform to a second level, overlapping with the former yet autonomous in turn.

This hybrid configuration, emerging from the interrelation between globality—the systematized—and particularity—the 'characteristic'—would also frequently translate as a calculated use of disparate building materials (concrete, brick, heavy materials, in continuous socles; wood, metal sheeting, light materials in the juxtaposed structures), favoring a certain dual perception, ambiguous and hence subtly discomforting, of the project.

SYSTEMS WHICH ARE, IN ANY EVENT, PARTICULARLY VERSATILE PRECISELY BECAUSE OF THEIR MIXED CHARACTER, AIMED CLEARLY AT MAKING THE SYSTEMATIC COMPATIBLE WITH THE SEEMINGLY ALEATORY.

Ⓗ Steven Holl. Makuhari (1994-96) Foto: Paul Warchol

① Eduard Bru & OAS. Cerdanyola, Barcelona, 1994

③ MVRDV. Wozoco building (Amsterdam 1996) Photo: Jordi Bernadó

Ⓡ Willem Jan Neutelings. Prinsenhoek building (Sittard, 1992-95)

© 1. Kas Oosterhuis. apartment building in Groningen (1995-96)
2. Willem Jan Neutelings. Scheme for Ghent (1996-97) Photo: K. Zwarts

Ⓜ Lacoste-Robain. Apartment building in Paris (1992)

EDUARD BRU
OAS

Housing Complex

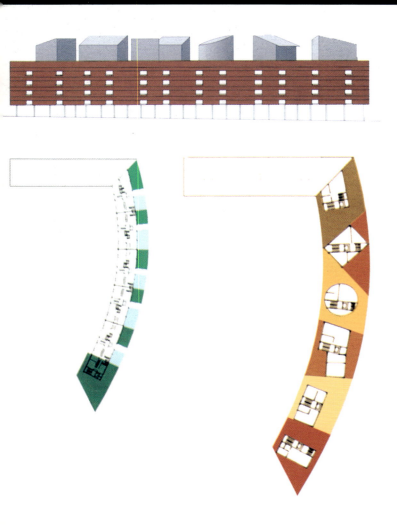

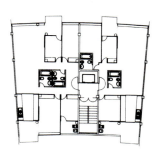

The project had to fit the criteria laid out by the PERI (local redevelopment plan) for the southern sector of Cerdanyola. The subject was of particular interest for four reasons. First of all, it was a brief for subsidized housing, a particularly ignored theme for architecture in the last decade. The other three reasons all arise from the site and the conditions of place —the houses, right beside major regional communication systems: the railway, the A-18 motorway, the new Sant Cugat-Cerdanyola road and the Barcelona-Manresa road; the natural setting, the morphology of the site, of particular interest in that it forms part of the valley of the Sant Cugat creek and provides a positive natural setting; the perimeter of the site, characterized by the occupation of the hill tops by single-family homes.

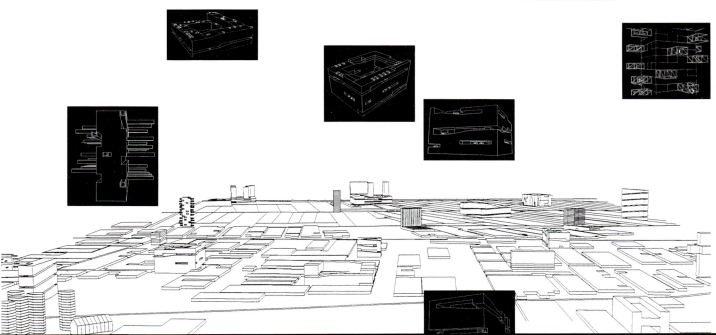

NL ARCHITECTS — Pixel City

Pixel City postulates a repertoire of huge buildings, a residential strategy applicable to any site whatsoever. Concentrating the built mass in a series of dense bodies conserves the specificity of the existing landscape, accommodating up to 7000 dwellings per enclave.

reference **Open Spaces**

enclaves

main idea **Landscape**

grounds

key concept **Manipulated Voids**

top: A. Debarre, P. Hannetel
Gironde Park, Coulaines (France)
bottom: Zuid-Flevoland (1991)

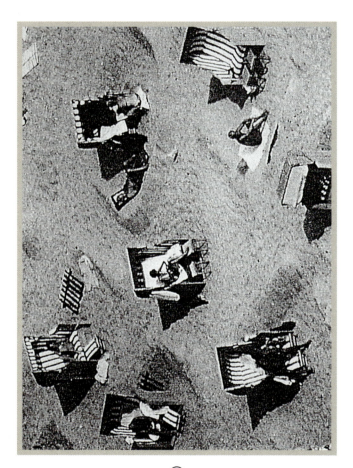

Ⓑ

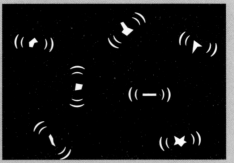

Ⓐ Elliot Erwitt. Simulation of a nuclear attack in a defined space (*Magnum Landscape*, Phaidon, London 1996)

C.1. ENCLAVES: fields, hollows, mattings

If the colonization of the territory has traditionally been centered on the implantation of 'built figures defined against a background landscape'—in the words of the architects NJIRIC & NJIRIC[43]—the consideration, today, of the 'void' as 'architectonic material' of the first order (not so much for its eventual 'natural' value as for its important spatial quality when it comes to eliciting ample orthogonals, visual apertures, horizontal dimensions, etc.) brings with it the obligation to invent new forms of intervention. In effect, empty space reveals itself to be a basic instrumental factor precisely because of

ITS 'VACANT' QUALITY; A 'SPACE IN NEGATIVE' CONSISTING OF ABSENCES MORE THAN PRESENCES

Ⓑ Spontaneous occupation of a surface (cf. *Arch+* 121, 1994)

Voids, 'operative dissipations of the built mass', interpretable as open force fields in which the new systems of occupation would have to refer to gentle tactics of colonization akin to those developed, for example, in traditional agrarian structures of occupation.

HOLLOWS OF INSERTION IN A 'DENTED' LANDSCAPE,

following guidelines no longer linked to constructed or urban geometries, but more organic, quasi-spontaneous, in form: mechanisms of infiltration and dispersal which would show an interest in colonizing the landscape, preserving its most marked qualities (the presence of large surface areas, the value of horizons and skies, the importance of the open terrain, the role of vegetation) by means of well-defined and dispersed enclaves, sufficiently distant from each other as to be unified solely by the very 'nature' that surrounds them.

43. Cf. NJIRIC & NJIRIC: project statement for Glasgow, *Europan IV* catalog, Europan, Paris, 1996.

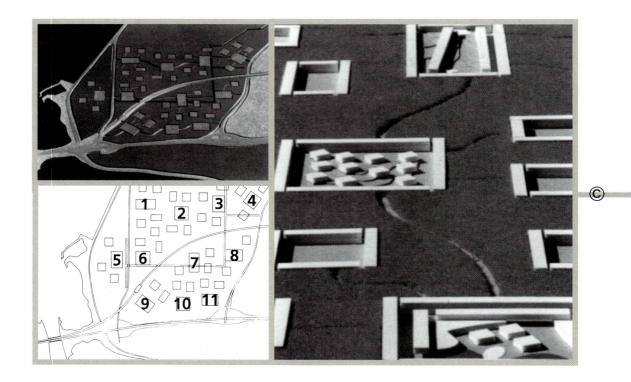

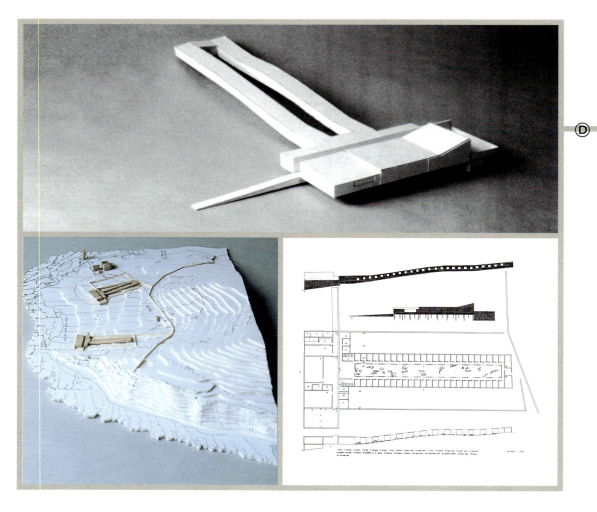

'FIELDS WITHIN FIELDS', FUNCTIONAL 'CARPETS' SLIPPED INTO THE LANDSCAPE. Operative landscapes are landscapes capable, in part, of traducing an appropriation of the terrain through the minimalized dispersal of its elements into subtle relationships balancing occupation and distance. The experiments of Land Art would not be foreign to this benign notion of acting on empty space, based on the idea of strategic 'incisions' in the landscape, in which the number, density and the distance between interventions would be seen to be basic.

The proposals of **TAKEO OZAWA** for the suburban area of Almere (1995), and above all those of **NJIRIC & NJIRIC** for Glasgow (Europan IV, 1996), propose similar strategies by using systems based on the definition of 'small artificial hollows' inserted into a host landscape (a variation, once more, on the commensalist theme). The natural landscape would appear, however, as a single barely-modified space, not divided into plots but merely appropriated from low-density enclaves molded and adapted to the terrain (one might point to the trench work in the first case, and to the delicate excision work in the second), configured as superposed artificial 'layers' slipped into the landscape receiving them. **TONY FRETTON**'s project for a residential reception center in Tibet also deals with the implicit question—how to build on a certain scale in surroundings which ought, for the most part, be preserved—through the designing of a series of 'habitational mattings', consisting of small built volumes and interior gardens, in which the profiles of the building mutate into huge walls inserted into the terrain.

In all these cases it is a question of an 'atomized order' which would ultimately refer the proposals to new processes of colonization and management of the territory.

In that sense **TROTTIN-MARIN**'s project for the respecification of the open spaces of the Grande Synthe housing estate (Europan III, 1994) proposes less a design scheme than a cost-effective system for the anonymous emptiness, by restructuring it into working gardens or allotments as a potential way of providing for the vital maintenance—given individual initiative—of large 'interland' spaces. A system open, therefore, to diverse, variable and heterogeneous landscape configuration, supported solely by the effective definition of the new plots and, in this case, by the scheme for a small prototype: a pavilion which, as a dismountable, transportable and ephemeral elementary structure, would guarantee not only an exterior, 'disconnected' amplification of the limited mass housing which characterizes the sector but a reversible instrument for occupation of the interstitial void.

Following on from this, one might emphasize the possibilities inherent in this notion of reversibility, associated here with the idea of the pavilion as a small 'infiltrated' enclave. Constructions generally based on light structures (huts, sheds, containers, kits, etc.) of elementary, quasi-abstract form which **WOULD CONSTITUTE A POTENTIAL REPERTOIRE OF 'MUTE', 'AUTISTIC' OBJECTS, MERELY 'DEPOSITED'** in the landscape, with no wish to make geometric or volumetric interventions in places where the characteristics of natural space do not invite change.

© Takeo Ozawa. Project for the suburban area of Almere (1995). Dispersed fields of occupancy and detail of colonizable gaps

© Tony Fretton. Reception center in Tibet (1994). Plan, section and details of the general model and of one of the enclaves

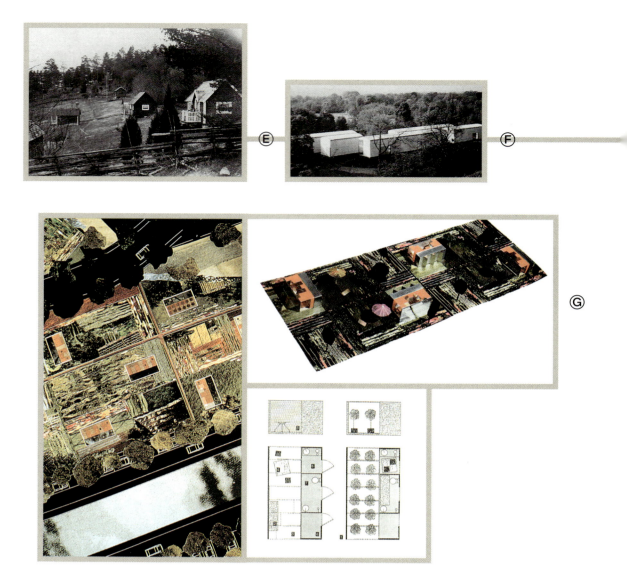

86

THE OLD URBANIST DICHOTOMY BETWEEN 'URBANIZABLE' AND 'NON-URBANIZABLE' AREAS WOULD THUS GIVE WAY TO VARIED AND SIMPLE STRATEGIES OF COLONIZATION OF THE LANDSCAPE, ACCORDING TO THE SPECIFIC VOCATION OF THE SITE;

strategies, even, which in certain situations would eventually place in crisis the idea of permanent property (and construction) on the territory (and thereby the implicit desire to underline, through 'stable' figuration, the real-estate value of the ground, substituting it by other kinds of models founded on a mild and reversible occupation of the landscape, capable of admitting temporary, 'precarious' uses).

The 'magic boxes' designed by ÁBALOS-HERREROS in their 'AH' project express this idea of generic contract with the landscape by means of a new notion of inhabiting: their artefacts are technical elements 'as might be a tractor, a combine-harvester or a tanker truck.'[44] They do not seek to compete with the landscape, but instead 'to traduce the lesser stability and greater fugacity of man's life and the habits that surround him.' Proceeding from similar premises, one might point to the works of the ACTAR group, oriented, in their MOAI project (a Spanish acronym translating as 'Optional Interurban Housing Module'), towards the investigation of tactical mechanisms of residential and landscape colonization capable of favoring reversible and non-aggressive occupations of the landscape, both in those areas of important urbanistic and environmental value like the Son Espanyol zone, siting of the future Parc Bit (Majorca, 1993), a large data processing center in direct relation with its surroundings and in which the residential zone would be appointed by means of a strategic dispersal of small individual hollows with built housing hidden away among the vegetation–as in those apparently unprofitable spots, as far as traditional urbanism is concerned (flyovers, quarries, marginal ground, old service structures, marshes, reserves of disused agricultural land, etc.), strategically recyclable and conducive to alternative residential models of a temporary nature, or of rehousing schemes in conflictive and crisis conditions (cf. chapter II). Models, in any event, which would imply the ability to act by starting from the mutability, ephemerality and aleatoriness of a culture itself open to mobility, precariousness and the rapid amortization of objects and events.

44. cf. ÁBALOS & HERREROS: project statement, in Quaderns 210, 1995 and Quaderns 213, 1996.

Ⓔ Colonization through occupancy and physical distance

Ⓕ Pavilions for Documenta, Kassel

Ⓖ Trottin-Marin. Proposal for restructuring the open spaces of Grande Synthe (Europan III, 1994). General plan and detail of model and of the prototypes of rapid colonization

Ⓗ Ábalos-Herreros. AH House, 1995. Industrialized housing units for a generic contract with the landscape

Ⓘ 1. Parc Bit 1993. General plan, model and view of the buildings among woods.
2. ACTAR Arquitectura. MOAI system (Optional Interurban Housing Modules)

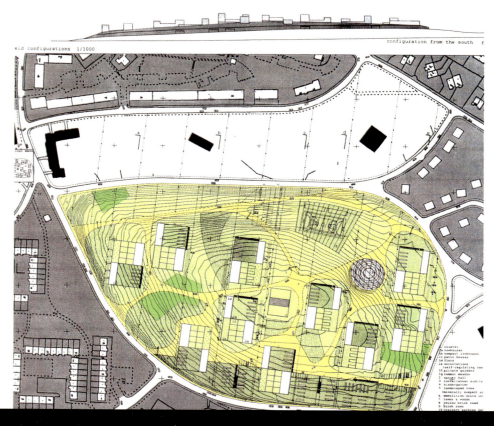

NJIRIC+NJIRIC

Atom Heart Mother

General plan
View of the whole
Pixels

A coherence of interfering site complexities, a reaction to the severe social context, psychodelia of suburban and protection needs

DIGITALIZATION OF THE FIELD
The disappearance of hierarchy implies a transformation of the figure/background ratio towards the coding of both, as well as field/field ratios.

SUSTAINABLE DEVELOPMENT
As a general housing strategy: radical urbanism + (possible) common development.
The houses—as simple as they ever were the new neighbourhoods—complex and open, redefine the collectivity.

Europan 4, Glasgow, Competition 1996, 1st prize

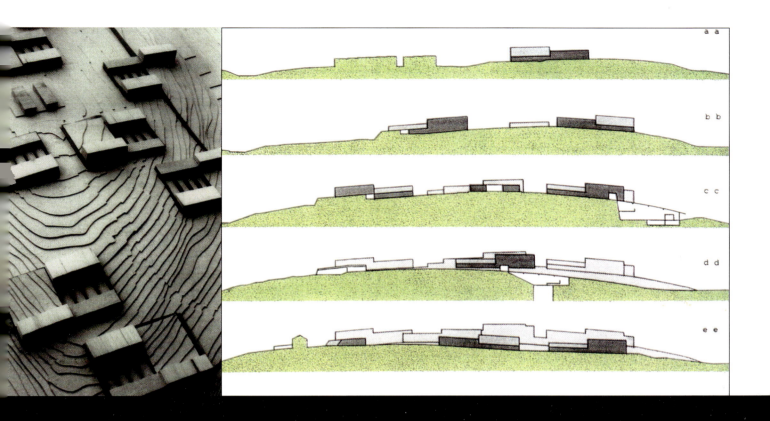

ARCHITECTURE AS A PROCESS:
a. A densification over time (i.e., birch planting starts simultaneously with the demolition)
b. Programmatic tides (day/night or summer/winter rhythm).
TIME-SCHEDULED LANDSCAPING
As a possible policy for environmental improvement of former mining sites
DECOMPOSITION OF MIDDLE-CLASS NEIGHBOURHOOD =
putting the existing typologies into new congested relations (like a lap-top PC). Iterating the 'new neighbourhood' tradition Radburn, Harlow, Cumbernauld, Milton, Keynes, Priesthill Porosity + local interconnectivity =
 a shift from physical to virtual "gardens" (based on affection and mutual understanding)–
non–hierarchical condition of neighbourhoods

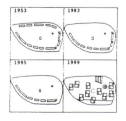 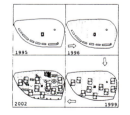 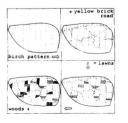

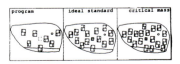

Model detail
Adaptation of enclaves to the terrain, in section
Conceptual ideograms
Plan: detail of various enclaves

B

C

D

E

F

90

 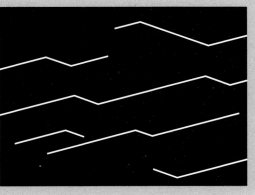

Ⓐ Kuwait: trench terrain during the Gulf War (archive photo)

C.2. TERRAINS: contours, trenches, grounds

In other methodologies an intervention in empty space would call for unusual and heterodox variables: systems resulting from direct work on the already architectonicized ground, the valorization of emptiness as a 'space in negative', understood here in relation to its more topomorphic manifestations: dunes, reliefs, mattings, trenches, folds, etc., as metaphorical figures of a potential artificial geography not so very far—in its spatial imaging— from the one that is more natural. A 'figured void'[45] in which the work would no longer be carried out from the prioritized configuration of the mass as constructed in height—architecture as 'edification'—but instead from the restructuring of the horizontal superfice; functional voids in locations of frequently conflictive reality.

Topographies versus typologies

PROJECTS BASED, THEN, ON THE ARTIFICIAL 'MODELLING' OF THE GROUND PLANE, AS A WAY OF ENDOWING THE SITE WITH NEW CONTOURS,

by means, even, of 'negative' changes—excavations, trenches—that run counter to orthodoxy; artificial, 'mineral' terrains which would nevertheless demonstrate their vocation for manifesting themselves as 'landscapes'.

Dislocation, the theoretical proposal formulated by **KATSUHIRO ISOBE** for the riverbanks of the South Axis (Amsterdam, 1995)—and related to some of the recent researches undertaken by **HERMAN HERTZBERGER**, notably in his Urban Development Plan for Freising (1993)—probes that possibility of imposing 'geomorphic' order, defined here as the relief lent by the roofing: a rhythmic sequence of undulating excisions—akin to artificial dunes—and alternating free-form excisions permits the accommodation of, respectively, residential programs and open spaces given over to individual patios and gardens, thus retaining the landscape character of the surroundings.

Ⓑ Honnan, Shansi, Shensi and Kansu. Dwellings excavated in the loess

Ⓒ Glasgow, 1993 Photo: Margherita Spilutini

Ⓓ Luminous web above the terrain (Berlage Institute exercise, 1994)

Ⓔ Incisions: *Land Art* interventions in Dutch river infrastructures

The terrain as a support for different uses
Ⓕ Access ramp to the parking area of the Plaza de España (Girona). Architects: Martínez Lapeña-Torres, 1991 Photo: Esther Rovira

45. Cf. PELLISSIER, Alain: 'L'Invention du paysage,' in *Europan III*, op. cit.

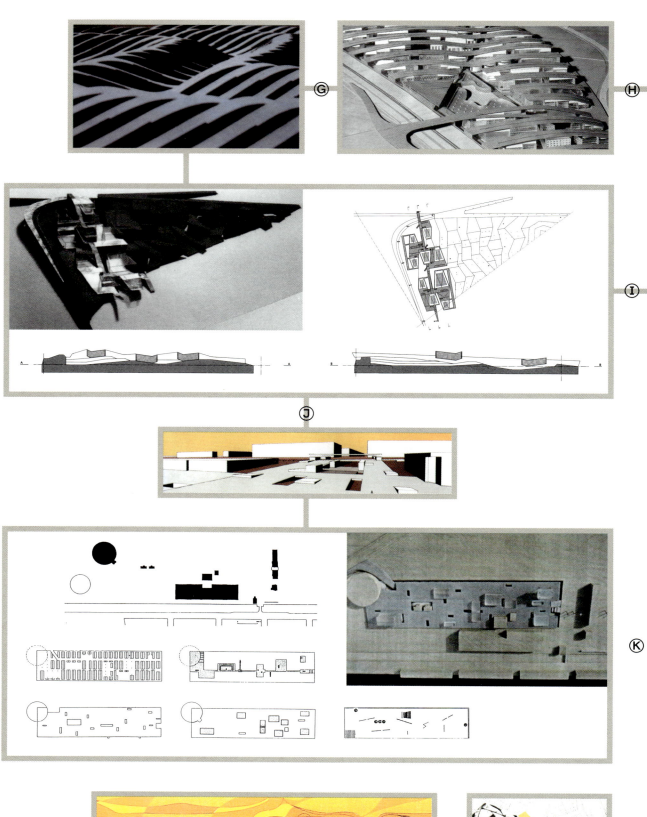

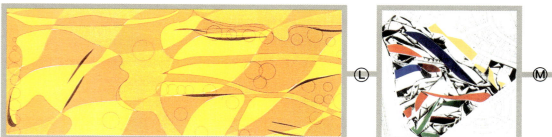

In other examples, like 'Folding', **ELLEN MONJEN**'s proposed development for Zuidlaren, or that of **NJIRIC & NJIRIC** for Den Bosch and Schwering (Europan III, 1994), the quality of the 'artificial void' would proceed from the idea of large, free platforms with strategic incisions, rhythmic slashes intended to accommodate trench-like programs, so establishing a first set of references (configured as a huge traversable void) punctuated by occasional excrescences intended to provide access to the private spaces (English patios, gardens, squares, etc.) and to the mixed programs situated on a lower level. The **DIACOMIDIS-HARITOS-NIKODIMOS-PAPANDREOU** team's proposal for Meyrin (Europan III, 1994) studies this type of scheme in depth through the development of three levels, rhythmically incised to form a crystallized landscape of folds and inclines which would correspond to the roofs of a large parking space, a space of mixed use, and an area intended for low-level housing formulated, here too, as trenches. A similar approach to that taken by **KELLY SHANNON** in his 'Simulated Topography' project (Amsterdam, 1993), where here too the architectonic program ultimately disappears in a sea of inclined planes in movement: chiselled surfaces, ramps which slash the superficies, strategic penetrations of light allow him to define singular and manifestly non-tectonic landscapes.

Other projects, like those of **SORIANO-PALACIOS** for Bilbao (Europan IV, 1996), or **ACTAR** for Calella (Europan III, 1994), grow out of a rejection of the old regulatory structures imposed on the territory and try instead to emphasize the landscape possibilities inherent in the site itself: cuttings, undulations, seams, mineral strata are reformulated, therefore, by means of new geological forms, architectonic this time, irregular in texture, material and color, and considered more as 'stratigraphic incisions', as 'engravings' or 'geometric slippages' than as severely-built geometries. Pavement, vegetation, terrain, breaches and blocks combined in a new attempt to create mineralized, crystallized and intaglioed artificial landscapes, yet still connected to natural movements.

GEOGRAPHIES RATHER THAN ARCHITECTURES; geographies where the effectiveness of architecture would not reside in the stylistic definition of the built, but in the specific ability to propound a new 'topos' issuing from the fact that—as **YORGOS SIMEOFORIDIS** rightly points out [46]—'if in Europe it is contour—the architectonic presence—which traditionally determines urban physiognomy, then that "architecture of the facade", that predominance of form, is today confronted by another kind of tradition, a potential architecture of the terrain capable of privileging projects with fuzzy, ambiguous outlines, vague forms, a fluidity of exterior and interior space and contact with a nature formed precisely of those new and unwonted transitional spaces, both elastic and flexible, generated by the redefinition of contemporary open space and its relation to residential architecture.'

46. Cf. SIMEOFORIDIS, Iorgis: 'Tansiciones,' in *Quaderns* 211, 1995

Ⓖ Katsuhiro Isobe. South Axis (Amsterdam, 1995)

Modellings
Ⓗ Herman Hertzberger. Urban development plan for Freising (1993)

Reliefs
Ⓘ Kelly-Shanon. Simulated Topography (Amsterdam, 1993)

Reliefs/grounds
Ⓙ Dallas-Diacomidis -Haritos-Nikodimos -Papandreou (Meyrin–Europan II–1994)

Modellings

Ⓚ Ellen Monjen. "Folding" scheme, Zuidlaven 1994

Reliefs/intaglios
Ⓛ ACTAR Arquitectura. Scheme for Calella (Europan III, 1994)

Reliefs/intaglios
Ⓜ Soriano-Palacios. Scheme for Bilbao (Europan IV, 1996)

KATSUHIRO ISOBE

'Dislocation'

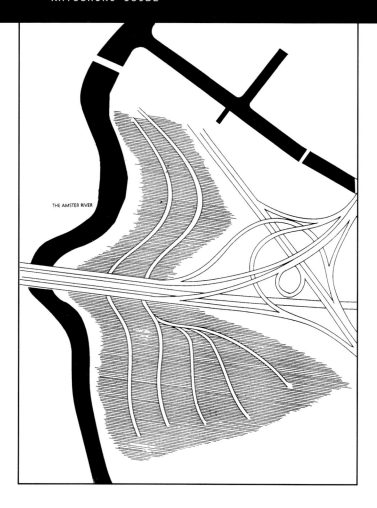

The edges of major roads often give rise to desolate expanses of space. This scheme tackles the transformation of such marginal spaces by means of an inhabitable topography, which serves as both barrier and river dike.

View at night
Detail view of the whole
Ground plans of setting

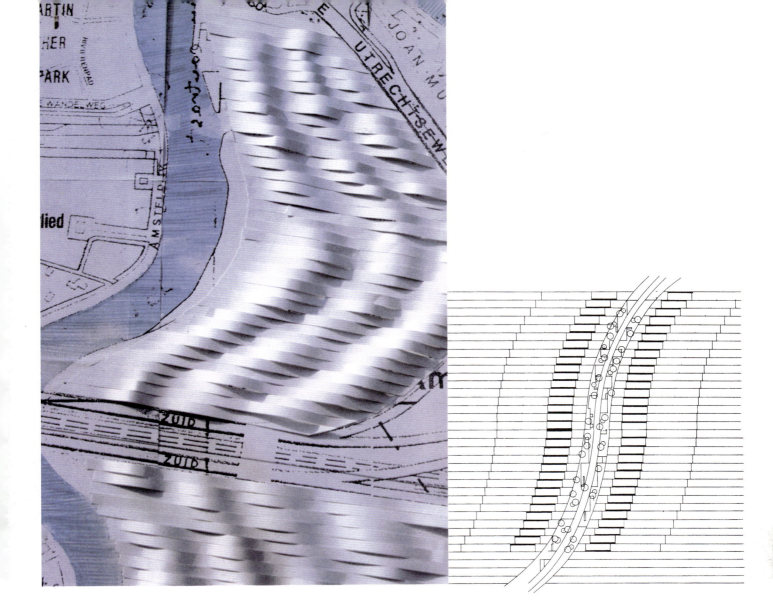
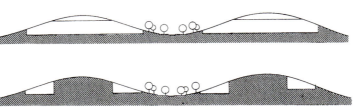

Housing along the south axis.
Amsterdam, 1993
(*The Berlage cahiers* 3, 1995)

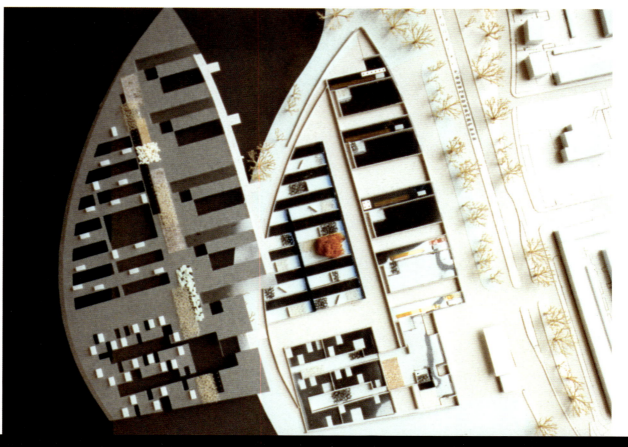

HELENA NJIRIC
HRVOJE NJIRIC

Structural dike

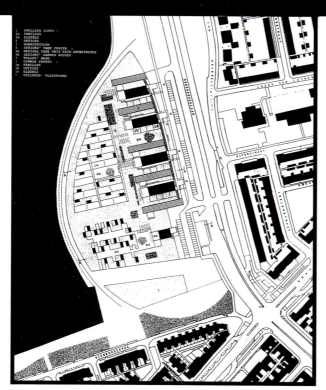

The project proposes a structure, and organization framework, which is a tripartite scheme:
1. of small structures, solitary and transparent, in the first row, conceived as a semi-propulsive membrane (entrances to the patios and the dwellings, placed on a lower level)
2. of perpendicular bars in the second row forming blocks of symmetrical houses (bars of dwellings)
3. a row of lower units, forming a kind of protective shield against the traffic (a row of conservatories).
The ensemble is conceived as a repetitive structure of base units: a bar of dwellings, a thicket of work areas and rows of tulips and bands of houses with gardens. A structural unit. Ground floor / upper floor plan.

Den Bosch. Winner.
Europan 3, 1993

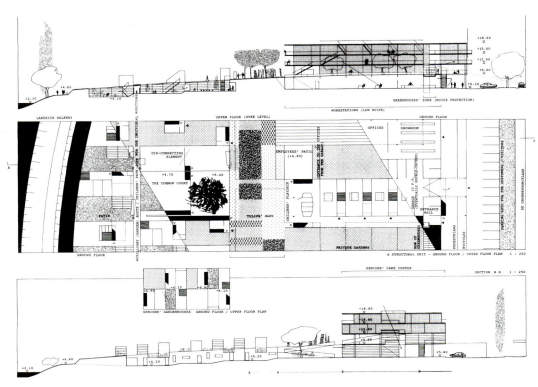

A structural unit. Ground floor/upper floor plan.
Cross sections A-A and B-B

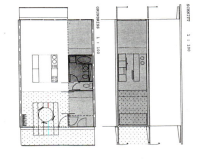

Models of inhabitation

reference **Consolidated Fabrics**

main idea **Dilation**

key concept **Incisions / Excisions**

'Berlin'. Photos Ramon Prat

Ⓑ

Ⓒ

Ⓓ

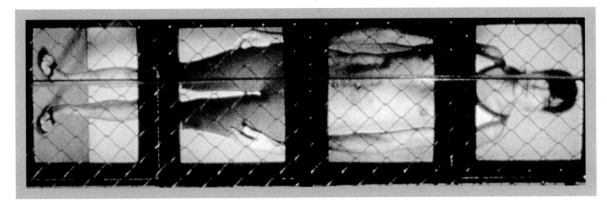

INCISIONS/EXCISIONS: joints, breaches, abuttals

Proceeding from this notion of the 'void' as an active mechanism with a restructuring capacity, it is useful to reflect once again, as a brief corollary, on the historical city, on those fabrics traditionally based on continuity and accessible today in terms of new, intuitive experiences emerging from other, less coherent settings. Intuitions which would signal the necessity for revising the old idea of the 'center' as no longer being a 'congealed' historical landscape, but rather a site potentially open to operations of redefinition based more on the action of the new mechanisms than on the evocation of old-fashioned attributes.

MECHANISMS CAPABLE OF FAVORING A NEW ROLE FOR THE RESIDENTIAL PROJECT IN SETTINGS WHICH ARE STILL TOO SACRALIZED

(yet, for all that, no less subject to profound material and functional tensions), in which housing all too often has tended to play the mere role of figurative recreation. Mechanisms which, when faced with various borderline situations of congestion and compression, would have had dilation and distortion as their principal methodology.

Mechanisms open, then, to discontinuity and evanescence; that is, to an interpretation of emptiness, not just as absence, but also as syncope –an interval or space of interruption– capable of generating new relationships between fabric and object[47]. **ACTIONS UNDERSTOOD LESS AS THE CONTINUITY OF THE FABRIC THAN AS ITS MERE ASSEMBLY.** Narrow cells, for instance, plain in aspect, introduced in a consolidated mass in which the added element would be reduced at times to an open union, a clamp, between solid built structures whose connection would remain secure—as **JOS BOSMAN** rightly points out[48]—thanks, paradoxically, to the immaterial, autistic character of the new intervention (the stability of which would logically depend in turn on the parts of the fabric it keeps optically unified).

Ⓐ 'Union joints'. Fragments of bodies 'united' by brief syncopes

Ⓑ Herzog & de Meuron. Schützenmattstrasse building (Basel 1993) Photo: M. Spiluttini

Ⓒ Claus en Kaan. Housing block in Amsterdam (1994)

Ⓓ Waro Kishi. Blue House (Osaka 1989)

47. Véase los números de *Quaderns* 202 (Estenosis) y 203 (Dilataciones) dedicados al tema.
48. Véase BOSMAN, Jos: "Nueva arquitectura neofuncional," *Quaderns*, 202 (1993).

E

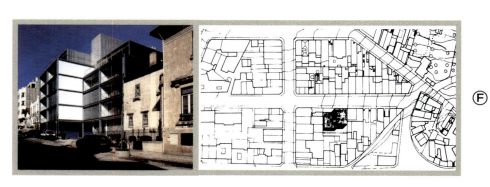

F

G

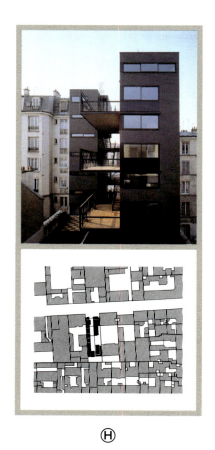

H

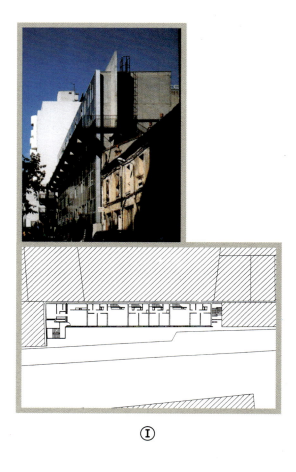

I

The well-known project of **HERZOG & DE MEURON** for Schützenmattstrasse (Basel, 1993)—an enormous vertical metal grille, a breach, a void organized in plan around a large central patio, a void in turn—or the single-family projects of **WARO KISHI**—especially his Blue and White Houses (Osaka, 1989 and 1992), two pure, 'functional' mechanisms organized around a free-form ground plan—would be paradigmatic of this ambivalent relation between fabric and object. Projects which are not imposed as new objects, but conceived, rather, as omissions, interruptions, dematerializations of the fabric: metaphorical voids intended, then, as devices capable of provoking vertical 'trenches' in landscapes that are congested, saturated by figurative solicitation, and which, faced with the routine acceptance of alignments, volumes and outlines, would sooner act from the redefining or reformulation of the constructed mass. A mass that is 'off-center', 'out-of-sync', 'semi-detached' from the contiguous physical elements, and creates new volumetric movements, atypical extensions, unexpected spaces of omission.

Proposals put forward in situations of extreme compression which would make projectural intervention into a simple act of 'abuttal'—like **FRANCIS SOLER**'s scheme in Belleville (Paris, 1993): a large plafond, a kind of 'absent' metal stockade placed against a party wall; or an incision, as in the case of **PHILIPPE GAZEAU** in Paris (1994).

The binary proposal of **EDUARDO SOUTO** in Oporto would also illustrate that desire for both a volumetric and semantic redefining of the fabric, which in the case of **JOSEP LLINÀS**' project for the Carrer del Carme (Barcelona, 1995) acquires a special dimension: it is not a question, in effect, of 'posing the problem of distanciation or acceptance of the specific morphological constants of the fabric', but rather a reflection on occupied and liberated space within an overloaded mass. The project corrects accepted commonplaces—elementary alignments and volumetries—in order to articulate not one great solid mass but three discontinuous volumes supported on a socle which rectifies the line of the facade, opening the street to sun, light and air. All that with the objective of improving the condition of the fabric through its very distortion: the utilization of discontinuity, but also of fragmentation, excision and, in the final analysis, of empty space as positive and active, rather than picturesque, elements.

A void—great or small, interior or exterior, public or private—conceived, in any event, as a constructed dilation of the fabric, apt to give rise to interventions aimed at restructuring the conflictive reality of various fabrics, and approachable only through operations of infiltration and modelling—similar to those produced in the open landscape—of a landscape which is mineral this time, yet also subject to that fragile balance between action and perturbation characteristic of the surroundings themselves.

Ⓔ Paillard-Jumeau-Schmitt. The zip-fastener strategy. A way of infiltrating the fabric (Meaux 1994)

Ⓕ Eduardo Souto de Moura. Housing in Oporto (1995). Photo: Luís Ferreira Alves

Ⓖ Josep Llinàs. Housing in the Carrer del Carme (Barcelona 1995). Photo: Jordi Bernadó

Ⓗ Philippe Gazeau. Housing in Paris (1994). Photo: J.M. Monthiers

Ⓘ 1 & 2 Francis Soler. Housing in Belleville (Paris 1993). Photo: N. Borel

VICENTE GUALLART — Plaza del Árbol

BUILDING

Valencia's Plaza del Arbol—more street intersection than tree-lined square—is situated in the center of the old Arab quarter, with buildings in a state of ruin or semi-ruin and lacking in historical or architectural value. To try and create a square in such dense and chaotic surroundings seemed pointless. Nevertheless, the logical aspiration towards an exterior –public–space was arrived at some 14 meters above street-level in creating a large raised square which presents us with a new landscape and a new way of experiencing the old city. All housing is reached from the street below or from its prolongation by means of interior corridors and suspended walkways.

HOUSING

Man can cut himself off from everything in the big city. Every house can be a mini-world unique to the individual. An automatically air-conditioned space with a lot of natural light, yet without being visible from the immediate surroundings. Connected at will with the external world through the television, the phone, the computer...

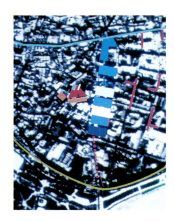

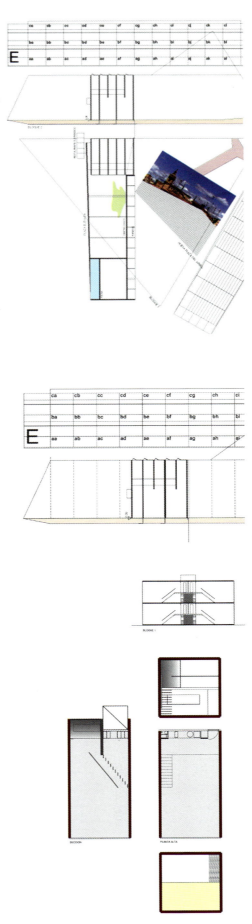

THE PROJECT AND THE SITE: REACTIVE MECHANISMS

In all probability, the greatest capacity for conceptual innovation in the majority of the proposals analysed is found, precisely, in that impulse to make a workable material out of conceptual abstraction, physical discontinuity and formal absence which combines a rigorously functional approach and a wilfully unprejudiced character, one ultimately indebted to the particular phenomena of metropolitan growth which involve the processes here discussed: phenomena in which the force of the detached and the just probable substitutes for the old inclination towards a nostalgia for the prefigured and the stable.

New modes of organization related to the movements of the contemporary city itself, which would see in the structuring capacity of **NETWORKS**, then, an order open to the presence of diverse events; and in the mingled configuration of its **DEVELOPMENTS** a heterogeneous and hybrid new definition of form, and in the idea of **INTERSTITIAL OPEN SPACE** itself the 'negative' potential of space.

An approximation to form made on the assumption of its theoretical state of latency within the framework of more global systems open to temporal processes; **NEW ORGANIZATIONS REFERRED, THEN, TO BASIC CONCEPTUAL SCHEMAS, TACTICAL DEVICES INTENDED TO PROMOTE CONFIGURATIONS WHICH ARE MERELY 'PARALYZED', BUT NOT FORCIBLY CLOSED OFF OR PREFIGURED.**

Interrelated devices which would define a 'project dynamics' rather than strict classifications—**DYNAMIC GUIDELINES (SEQUENCES-NETS), COMPLEX FORMATIONS (OUTBREAKS-MACULAE) AND MANIPULATED VOIDS (ENCLAVES-TERRAINS)**—whose major importance would no longer be rooted in their typification as eventual 'models', but instead in their capacity for dealing with concrete urban situations: infrastructural margins, boundary spaces, semi-natural landscapes, consolidated fabrics, etc.

THE READING ITSELF OF THE URBAN PHENOMENON GIVES WAY, THEN, TO A MORE CONCRETE ATTENTIVENESS TO THE SITE AS AN INCOMPLETE FRAME CRISS-CROSSED BY MULTIPLE SOLICITATIONS[49] and potentially open to new reactive mechanisms:

49. Cf. GAUSA & SALAZAR: 'Retráctiles,' op. cit.; and SOLÀ-MORALES, Ignasi: *Diferencias. Topografía de la arquitectura contemporánea*, op. cit. Photo: Ramon Prat

Reactive Mechanisms
which must be understood as restructuring methodologies attentive to the music of the specific, yet in syntony with a 'metapolitan' space in which the harmonious melody of a complete, prefigured, equilibrated city would have ceded to the evidence of a complex, overall score, but with an ultimately atonal, syncopated 'non-rhythm'.

Intrusive Mechanisms
infiltrated into reality; in strange complicity with the host space, not for provoking rejection, yet not necessarily in harmonious symbiosis with it.

Intersecting Mechanisms
which are autonomous and non-prejudicial, at times 'impertinent', sensitive to the projectural potential of 'suspense', to that fragile balance between nature and artifice, predictability and surprise, order and transgression, system and exception, control and chance characteristic of contemporary space.

Formal Mechanisms
generated from a strategic and structural—topological— approximation to the project. Immediate logics based on the intersection of energy, data, tensions, currents, flows and forces rather than figurations.

Perceptual Mechanisms
also aware of the potential of 'negative space', of the omission of the built, of interruption, discontinuity and the figurative syncope, of working with apertures, evaporations, ruptures, resections rather than with the pure geometry of the built.

Conceptual and Technical mechanisms

aware, lastly, of a dislocation of the traditional disciplinary factors intended to favor lightness and evanescence as against tectonicity, precision as opposed to massiveness, the abstract idea as opposed to the evocative reference, plastic expressivity (color, volume, informality, the value of the 'strange') as opposed to puritanically refined elegance.

Mechanisms, in any event, of a varied nature, but which would nonetheless rely on an optimistic approach to form

on the transformation, in fine, of a predictable or simply banal universe through the privileging of another one which is surprising, unpredictable yet suddenly more efficacious, fusing the conceptual rigor inherited from modernity with the expressive shock of contemporary perception itself into a single system. Manifestations as yet barely intuited, arising in direct response to the new parameters which today ground contemporary space, to that constant sensation of mutability which would already foreclose any notion of sedimentation. To those no longer comforting site-specific data. To the impossibility of hiding in typological models inherited from disciplinary orthodoxy. Or to the evidence of a necessary complicity with the materialization of a tattered and diffuse landscape completely open to the invention of the new, in which the strangely fragile nature of the emergent reality and the new conditions identifiable with it can be recognized.

WORKS

GEUZE · VAN BERKEL · MVRDV · NEUTELINGS · BRU · ACTAR ARQUITECTURA · DALLAS · DIAKOMIDIS · HARITOS · NIKODIMOS · PAPANDREOU

OPEN
SYSTEMS

ADRIAAN GEUZE
WEST 8

Borneo Sporenburg

Housing typologies with garden

Wall house

Emmenthal cheese

Drive-in

Court

Void

Big garden

▶ Location AMSTERDAM
Architects ADRIAAN GEUZE,
WIM KLOSTERBOER, YUSHI UEHARA,
SEBASTIAAN RIQUOIS
Developers NEW DEAL, STICHTING BO1,
SFB, SMITS BOUWBEDRIJF,
M.J. DE NIJS, PRIVATE
Design 1993 – Construction 1995-6

28-40 houses /Ha

100 houses /Ha

Borneo Sporenburg. 100 houses /Ha

Diagram showing principle for 'low-rise, high-density' typology

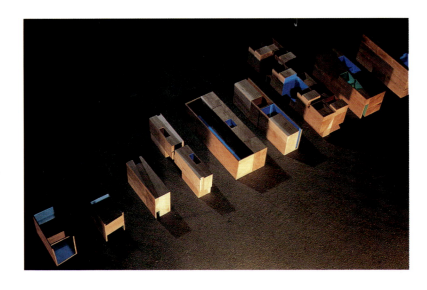

The project is a response to the demands of a large-scale residential operation 'on water', on two long peninsular wharves in Amsterdam's large port area. The proposal had to cover the location of 2500 housing units, representing a density of 100 homes per hectare, with the single family model predominating. The solution comprises the dynamic repetition of an abstract housing model.
Three superblocks are erected on this sea of habitable units: two of eight stories and one –'the chair'–of fourteen. They are responsible for providing a continuity with the surroundings, creating visual relations and 'telling a story' from far off. The 90 meter-wide Spoorweg canal flows between the two dykes. Two footbridges connect the two peninsular and two large green areas in the central zone, which stand in for the necessary absence of water amidst so many homes.
The apartments in the superblocks have a conservatory and covered balcony. Entrance to the rest of the homes is from the ground floor, which means a direct connection with the street and garden. The model, a free reinterpretation of the traditional Amsterdam house with frontage on the canal, inner courtyard and annexed buildings in the courtyard, makes this a new house-with-courtyard in strips with roof terrace; all in all, the operation is labyrinthine in character, like a kasbah, made up of courtyards and terraces.

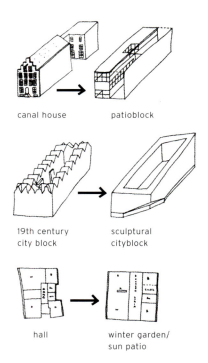

canal house → patioblock

19th century city block → sculptural cityblock

hall → winter garden/ sun patio

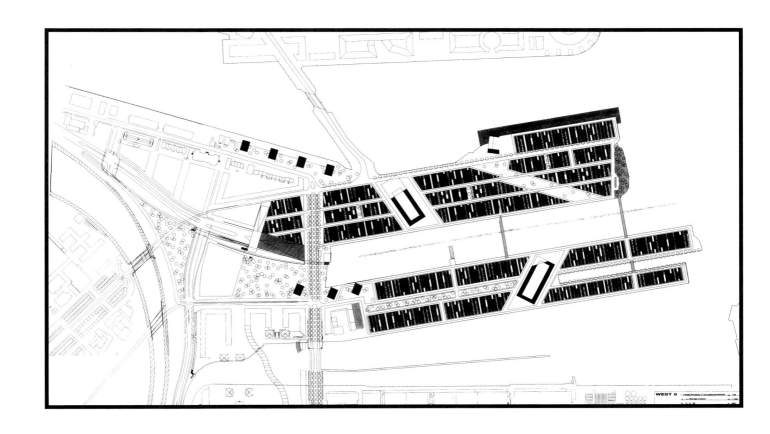

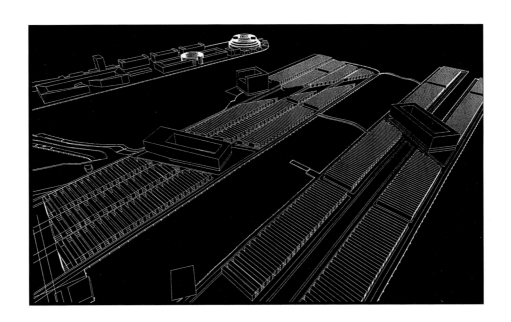

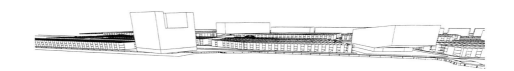

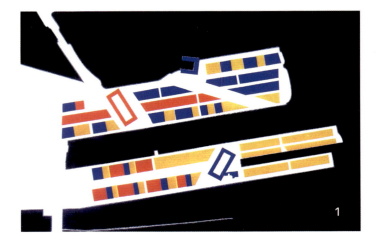

1. Program
2. Width of the plots
3. Clients
4. Differences in lifestyle
5. Architect's selection
6. Public space

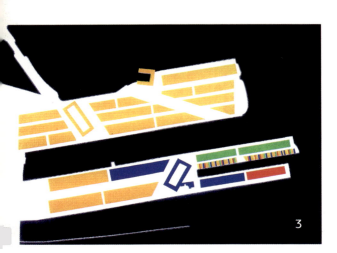
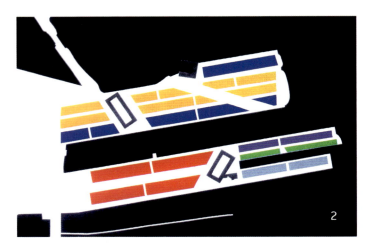

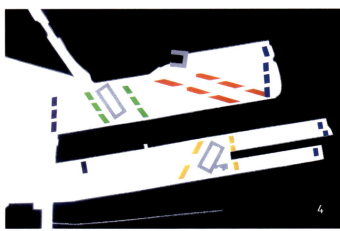
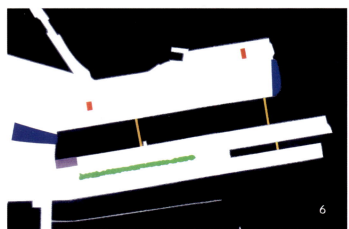

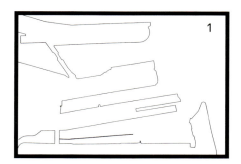
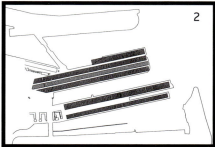
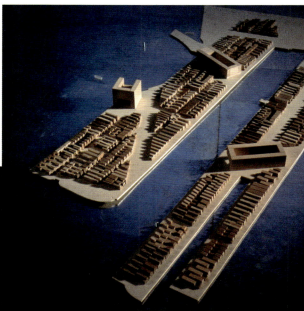

1. Structure of existing quays
2. Low-rise housing
3. The superblocks related to landscape
4. Superposition
5. Public space

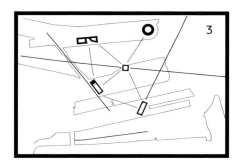
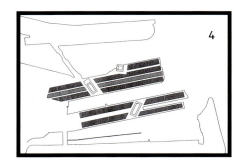

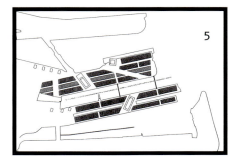

Participants

S. Beel, B. van Berkel, DKV, FARO, X. de Geyteer, Heren 5, S. Holl, Inbo, JA Atelier, F. Claus & K. Kaan, Marge, W.J. Neutelings, OMA, R. Petersma, Höhne & Rapp, M. Rohmer, Köther & Salman, Tangram, Van Sambeek & Van Veen, R. Visser, H. Zeinstra, K. Christiaanse, J. Herzog & P. de Meuron, LRRH, B. Mastenbroek & D. van Gameren, Van Herk & De Kleyn, J.L. Mateo, EEA, S. Sorgdrager, K. van Velsen, L. van der Pol, Tupker & Van de Neut, CASA, Van Goor, Stuurman & Partners.

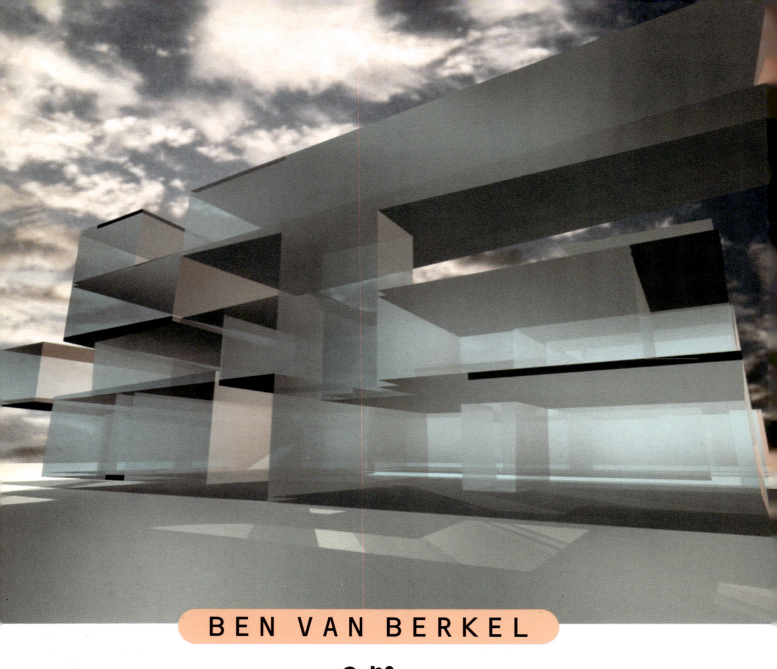

BEN VAN BERKEL

Borneo Sporenburg

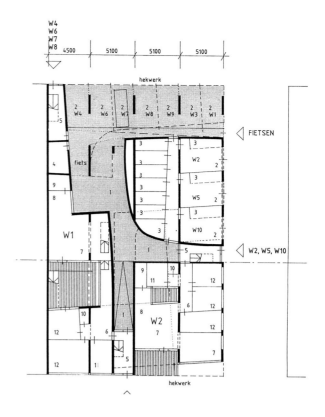
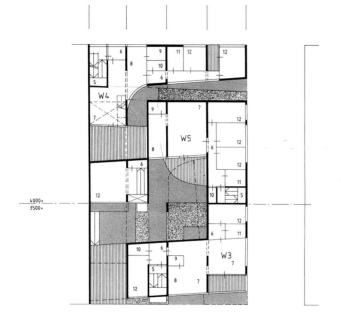

Block SP 15 D/52
Floor plans
1. Courtyard
2. Parking
3. Storage
4. Container room
5. Stairwell
6. Circulation space
7. Living room
8. Kitchen
9. Scullery
10. Toilet
11. Bathroom
12. Bedroom
13. Balcony
14. Terrace

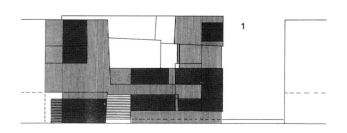

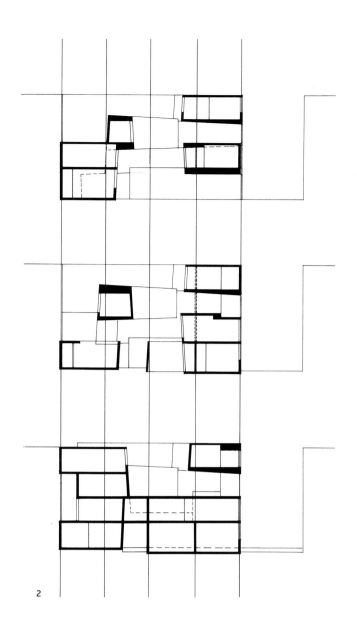

The plan for the Borneo Sporenburg district called for a dense network of small housing blocks. The design would be executed by some twenty different architects, fulfilling in each case virtually the same programmatic requirements. The two proposed blocks, only one of which is shown here, contain ten dwellings each. In the design process, differences between the two developed. They have been organized according to opposing principles. SP 15 D/52, which is in the middle of a row of buildings, has a central void, and the flats are characterized by intense spatial interrelations, while SP 17 B/58, which is on a corner lot, is more permeable to the exterior. All the entrances are located at the center of the block and the apartments at the edges.

Block SP 15 D/52
1. South elevation
2. Transverse sections
3. Longitudinal section
4. North elevation
5. East elevation

Location AMSTERDAM
Architect VAN BERKEL & BOS ARCHITECTUURBUREAU BV
Project team ROB HOOSTMANS, JEN ALKEMA, GIOVANNI TEDESCO, MARK DIJKMAN, CASPER LE FÈVRE
Design 1994

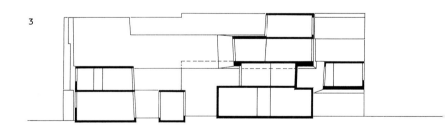

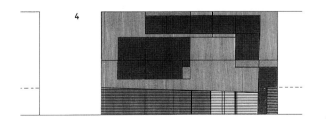

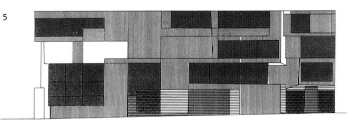

MVRDV

Hoornse Kwadrant

Location DELFT (NETHERLANDS) – Architects WINY MAAS, JACOB VAN RIJS, NATHALIE DE VRIES – Project 1996

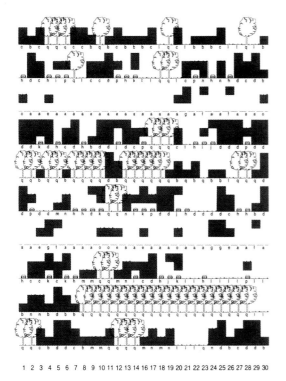
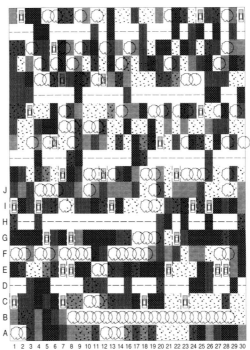

DIFFERENCE AS PARAMETER
What is striking about this project is the fact that, due to tight budgets for housing areas, the brief for these areas has been translated into an 'urbanism of percentages': the combination of economy and social obligation leads to strict maximum percentages for dwelling types (100 m² on three stories maximum, based on the ground), gardens (40 m² per house), parking places (1.2 cars per house), pavement (30 m² per parking place, including roads) and greenery (5 m² per house).
In order to address the demand for 'individuality' and 'variety' —seemingly the only and therefore overused architectural tools for mass housing—the given area has been organized by bands placed on the parking area, the one element with strict measurements.
By giving each band a different potential composition within the given and proposed, percentage-produced parts of the program, the clash of all bands—from the intelligent to the absurd—turns the built area into a kasbah-like labyrinth. The neighborhood acquires an adventurous quality, in which the 'unexpected' dominates.
To escape from the claustrophobic aspect of the resulting density, every dwelling has a tower-room or a patio and the public space has been given a hill, in addition to the supermarket and the sports hall, with a public view over this 'housing carpet' which stretches away towards the sea.

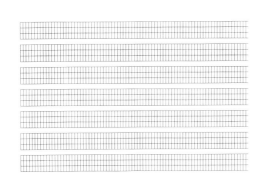
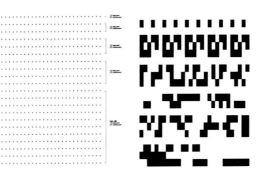

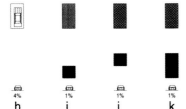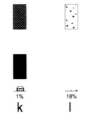

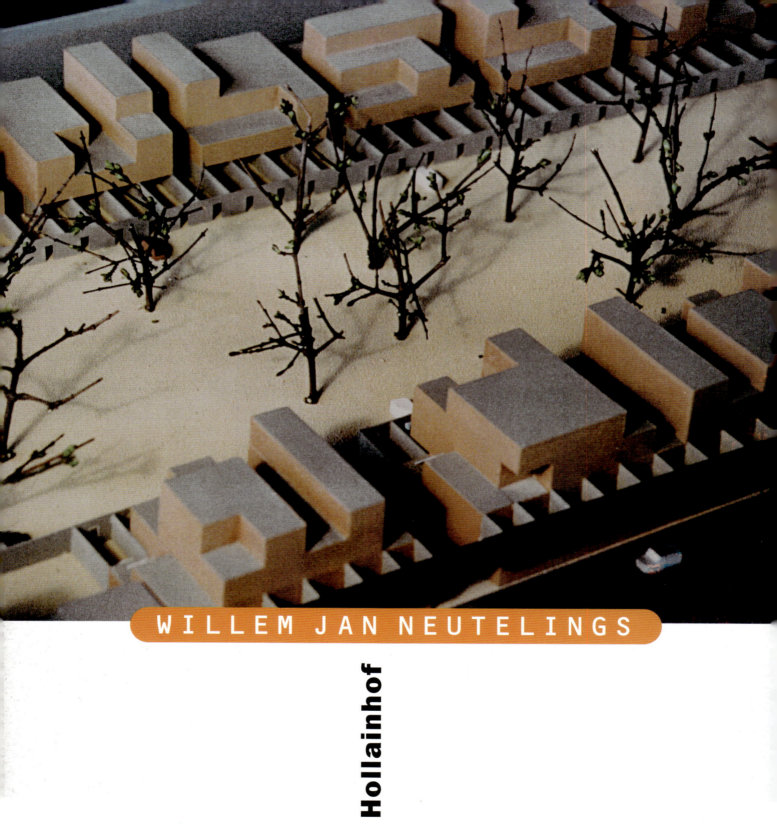

WILLEM JAN NEUTELINGS

Hollainhof

Elevations
1. Brusselse Poortstraat
2. Hollainhof east
3. Hollainhof west
4. River Schelde

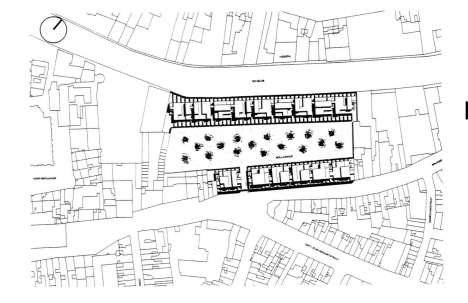

Location GHENT (BELGIUM)
Architect WILLEM JAN NEUTELINGS
Project team TADEJ GLAZAR,
FRANK HEYLEN, MECHIEL RIEDIJK,
KLAUS SCHLOSSER, JONATHAN WOODROFFE
Consultants BUREAU BOUWKUNDE,
DIK HOOGSTAD, RUUD GEHRING
Design 1993
Construction 1997

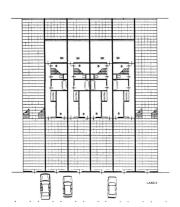 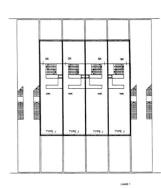 

Example of variation on levels 2 and 3

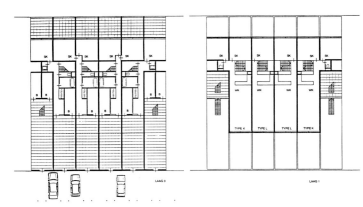 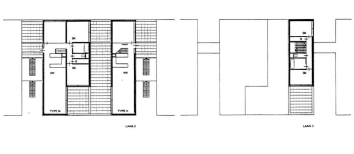

Riverfront housing units. Floor plans

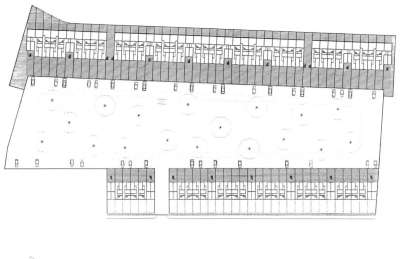

1

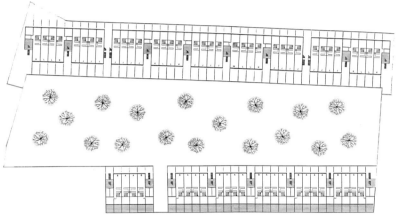

2

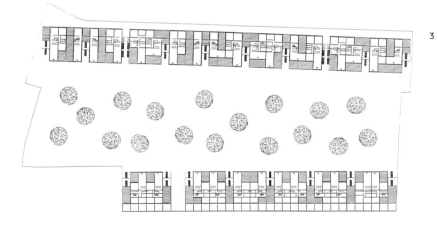

3

To establish a balance between intimacy and open space, between the individual and the collective, between a rural atmosphere and an urban setting: this was the premise for the combination of the small, strictly delimited private housing, maximized in its link to the interior and closed to the street. The houses are grouped in fifteen clusters which make up the urban front of the complex. Each cluster comprises a volume in the form of an unbroken plinth made up of four duplexes, and from two to four attic apartments, which are reached by an external stairway. The attics are laid out to create random variations on the strict party wall divisions of the lower houses. Privacy and flexibility of use were basic conditions in the design of the houses. This is the logic behind the bedroom area, which can be joined both vertically and horizontally to daytime activity spaces. The houses in the lower part, as well as the walls which separate the gardens, are of tinted concrete, and the upper units are clad with western red cedar. The conditions of the brief and budget are practically the same: there is no distinction between subsidized, private or rented housing.

General floor plans
1. Ground floor
2. First floor
3. Second floor
4. Third floor

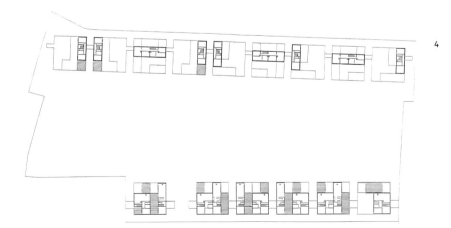

4

EDUARD BRU
SERRA-VIVES-CARTAGENA

Poblenou seafront

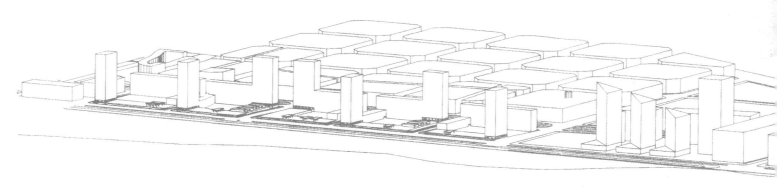

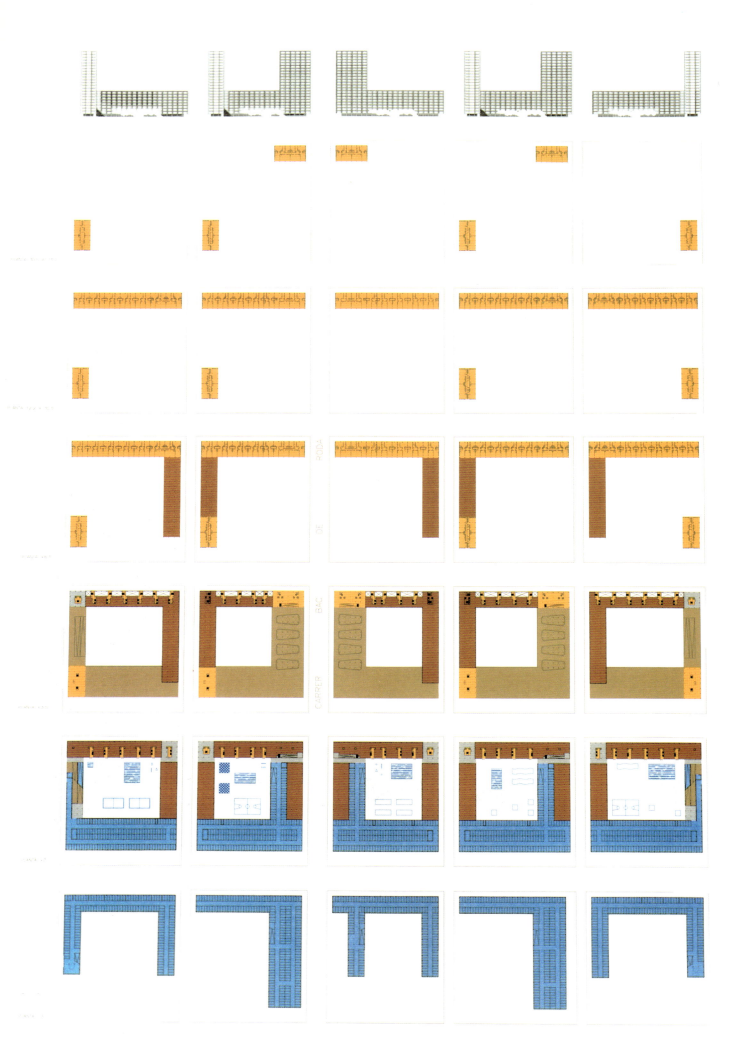

Location BARCELONA – Architects EDUARD BRU, ENRIC SERRA, LLUÍS VIVES, JORDI CARTAGENA – Collaborators M. L. FELIP, A. GARCIA, R. BIMBELA, N. LACOMBA (Architects) A. MARTÍNEZ, C. GELPÍ, M. MUÑOZ, L. GÓMEZ – Project 1995

The project for Poble Nou's seafront makes a contemporary intervention on the classical Cerdà block. This intervention in the Eixample is not taking place in a common-or-garden location, but on one of its edges: the seafront.
The very size that the city is acquiring, the presence of the two skyscrapers of Nova Icària, the project planned by the Kepro group, all consolidate a certain scale of response on the part of the city giving onto the seafront. Our project is situated precisely between two of these proposals on a new scale: the Olympic Village (Nova Icària) and the Kepro project (Diagonal Mar).
The project proposes two superposed sequences; one of aligned buildings and a second one of high buildings, which join up with their Kepro neighbours, the skyscrapers of Nova Icària and the face of Montjuïc. The principal view of these volumes is from an acute angle; they are designed as a succession which involves other events of the city and its landscape. They are not a diorama painted before the water, but a mechanism of relations between avenue, construction and landscape. Although they are meant to be interpreted in terms of the large scale, they keep within and scrupulously confirm the Cerdà plan, understood as a system of alignments and geometries which is living and transformable, that is, still useful today. By no means is it an attempt to indiscriminately fill the city's seafront with skyscrapers; they are situated according to spaced cadences which move closer together to point up an important urban event: the frontiers of the sector, the presence of the Bach de Roda axis.
Situated orthogonally to the first are more buildings of the same height and general character, though with different ground plans to suit the site. They follow Cerdà's alignment along the front, corresponding to the side of the waterfront promenade with which we are concerned.
In order to precisely create the geometry of the block, they extend its entire length, decreasing in height to that of the surroundings: in this way, 24-story blocks become continuous frontages of 10 floors. Seen from Bach de Roda, they look like a gateway between the city and the sea. Taken together, an urban profile which announces of the city to the seafront and vice versa, from the coast to the city. Low volumes join the two fronts, or delimit the third: they are used as businesses, offices or lesser modules of a residual nature. The fourth front, corresponding to the waterfront promenade, is left open and is public in character. It sets forward a symbiosis between the blocks and the promenade.
As originally proposed by Cerdà, the blocks become permeable where the presence of the more public elements calls for it. The whole is resolved in an emphatic continuity of volumes: a constructed mass which is emptied out or grows as required according to the –simultaneous–demands of a historical fabric and a living city. Altogether, it follows the alignments, safeguarding its own internal space, and opens out to the public and the sea. Each of the blocks is resolved individually but on the basis of common parameters, as part of a whole. Seen at a glance–the usual urban way of looking– the projected urban solution makes a turn: buildings all along the line of the coast with Montjuïc, the Olympic Village, Mar Bella…, and the same buildings cut off the Rambla on the front parallel with the water, turning Bach de Roda into a gateway, announcing the city. This turn –glancing along the coastline, turning your head and looking at the approaching city–is the heart of the project.

ACTAR ARQUITECTURA

Mixed residential mechanism

The site is a strange one: a part of the outskirts 'planted' in an engaging *fin-de-siècle* neighbourhood. A large, typically semi-urban piece of wasteland (lots carved up by forlorn fences, a grey supermarket, commercial warehouses, a disused factory, near to the train tracks...) stands out against a constellation of small, pleasant family houses and domestic buildings of a decadent, bucolic flavor, some of which are even lost in their own plot. The main attraction of the site lies in this unnatural cohabitation of scales and apparently discordant references. The aim is to look at both tensions, generating a mechanism which is sufficiently distant—and autonomous—to favor a tactical movement of appropriation in an extraneous space without references, but one which is also sufficiently ductile and flexible to harmonize with the specific elements which characterize the place: a rhythm—an infiltrator—which is capable of bringing into line the different vectors of force which cross here; strategic action rather than imposed order.

An elemental sequence of parallel lines, reinforced by the planned residential units, hatches the site like an abstract outline, a changing bar code. Rather than repetition, it is cadences that the system proposes, which are to be distorted and deformed according to the petitions and events—or accidents—which come to disturb the initial rhythm adopted. The residential units are variable: they may rise to three or four levels and house, on their ground floors, shops and services (with attics) of different shapes and sizes. A series of intrusive elements—free-standing, autonomous geometries—infiltrate their way in between. They may even include some of the small existing houses, ambiguously preserved by strategy or sentiment. The distribution of these counter-points allows the situation of various facilities and the articulation of the free space between blocks, taking the form of wedges of different colors, materials and textures (vegetable and mineral, natural and artificial). Occasionally the buildings will deform their basic volumetry, as well as their very outline, giving rise to a movement of distortion on the last two floors (set aside for loft spaces for a variety of uses), like a great animal turning its head to look at the sounds being made around it. The project is conceived, then, as the precise application of the ABC system intended by its authors, seen as a project based around the minimum housing requirements (70 m^2).

Starting out from three basic, prefabricated, modular elements (equipped walls) corresponding to the storage, bathroom and kitchen spaces, different spatial subtypes are generated; combinations generated by the strategic outline which sets out the equipped walls on each floor. On the facade, the changeable manifestations of each of the modules also produces a varying rhythm of differently-colored vertical edges to combine with the designed wall facings (glazed, opaque, fixed or sliding and protective) which enclose the space.

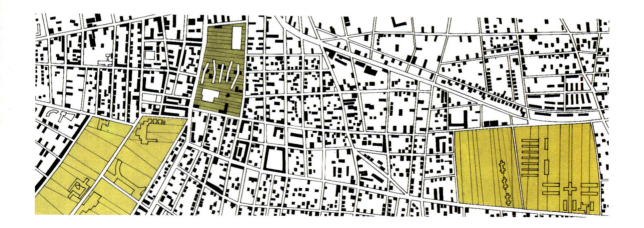

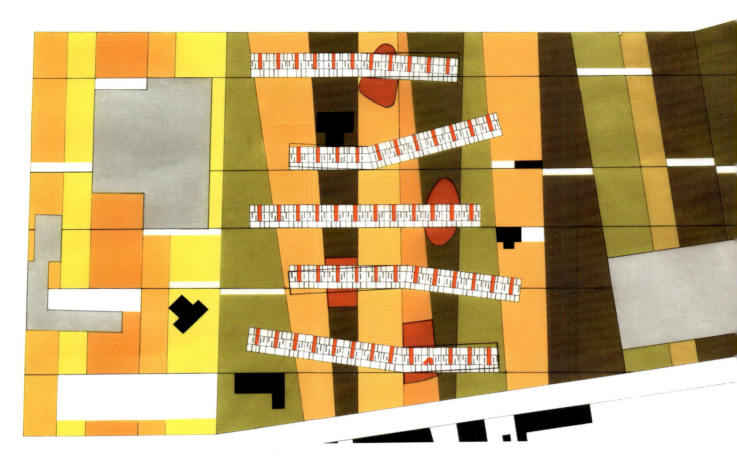

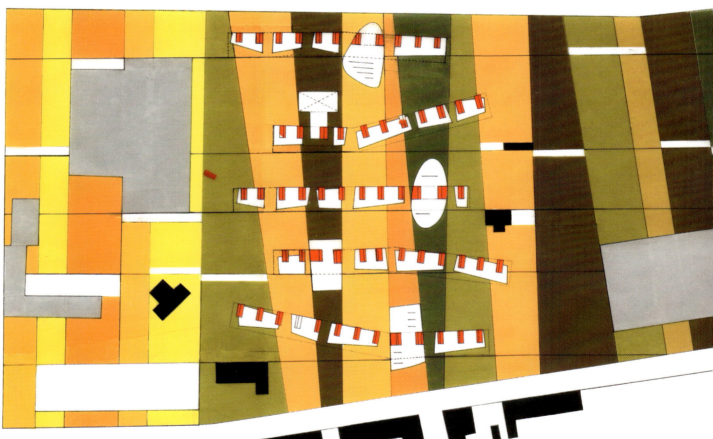

General layout of the complex. Ground floor and typical floor plans

Elevation

Floor plan, showing the ABC modular elements of storage, bathroom and kitchen spaces

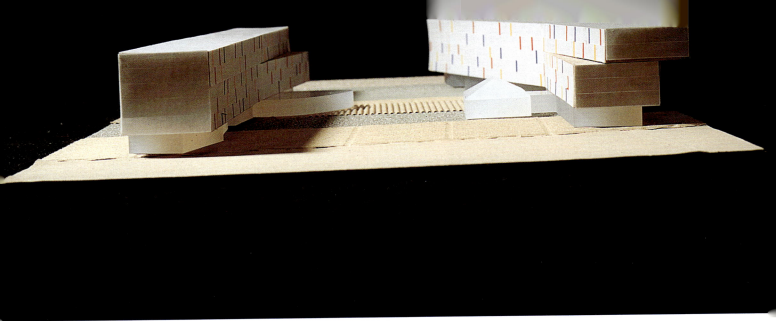

Location GRAZ (AUSTRIA) — Architects ACTAR ARQUITECTURA (MANUEL GAUSA, AURELI SANTOS, OLEGUER GELPÍ, IGNASI PÉREZ ARNAL, FLORENCE RAVEAU) — Collaborators JORDI CASTRO, CLIMENT GOMÀ, XAVIER RAMONEDA (Visual assistance) — Project 1996

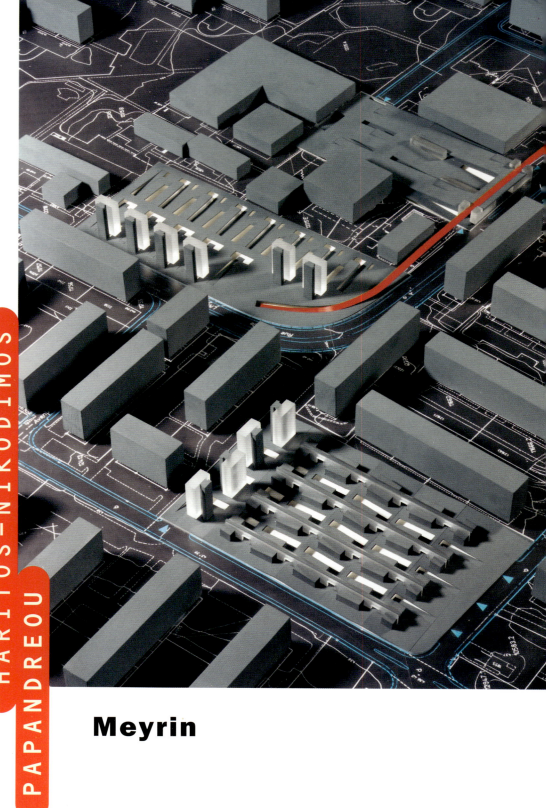

DALLAS–DIACOMIDIS HARITOS–NIKODIMOS PAPANDREOU

Meyrin

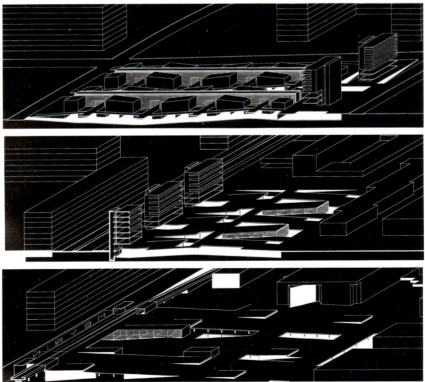

Location MEYRIN (SWITZERLAND) – Architects ALEXIOS DALLAS, CATERINA DIACOMIDIS, NIKOLAOS HARITOS, NIKOLAOS NIKODIMOS, KONSTANTINOS PAPANDREOU – Collaborators TASSOS MAGHIROS, SOPHIA VIZONITI

RENOVATION OF A HOUSING GROUP
1. Confronting the 'weak urbanity' of Meyrin, an emblematic town from the sixties, the project proposes a new artificial soil–a 'floating ground'– containing parking space, public space, street furniture, greenery, services, offices, housing, etc. This new artificial soil is structured on a human scale–perception, movement, transition, sense of 'belonging in a place'–without imposing other solid masses on the sector. It provides a new diffused urban landscape, 'an inhabited urban park'.
It proposes a possible strategy in remodelling problematic residential areas: the reappropriation of the infrastructural network and its restitution to the public realm.
2. This strategy is driven by a spatial module: the volume of the parking with a 5% slope, which according to traffic standards permits possibilities of parking, vehicle and pedestrian movement, offers interchangeability in terms of usage, distributing the density of the program at the three different sites, according to a repetitive yet flexible parcelling. The 5% slope makes an angled surface structure possible, facilitating both the connection and the development of the different spaces.
3. Three different platforms for social life take shape, each with a distinct urban quality:
a) The first (site A) ensures a correct transition from the proposed metro station and the parking lots to the shopping center. An 'intelligent void' responding to the climatic conditions and the everyday living habits of the place.
b) The third plateau (site C), devoted primarily to housing, explores the transition from the carpark to the housing unit (at home in town, in your car). Housing developed from the need for distributive flexibility, foreseeing the integration of teleworking in the apartment unit. Nature (trees, winter gardens) is considered to be a constituent element in this transition.
c) Due to its interlocking position along Rue des Boudines, the second plateau (site B) offers a filtered transition from the first site to the third site and vice versa. It contains several public facilities, parking, access to the school, the town hall, a shopping center, the cultural center currently under construction.

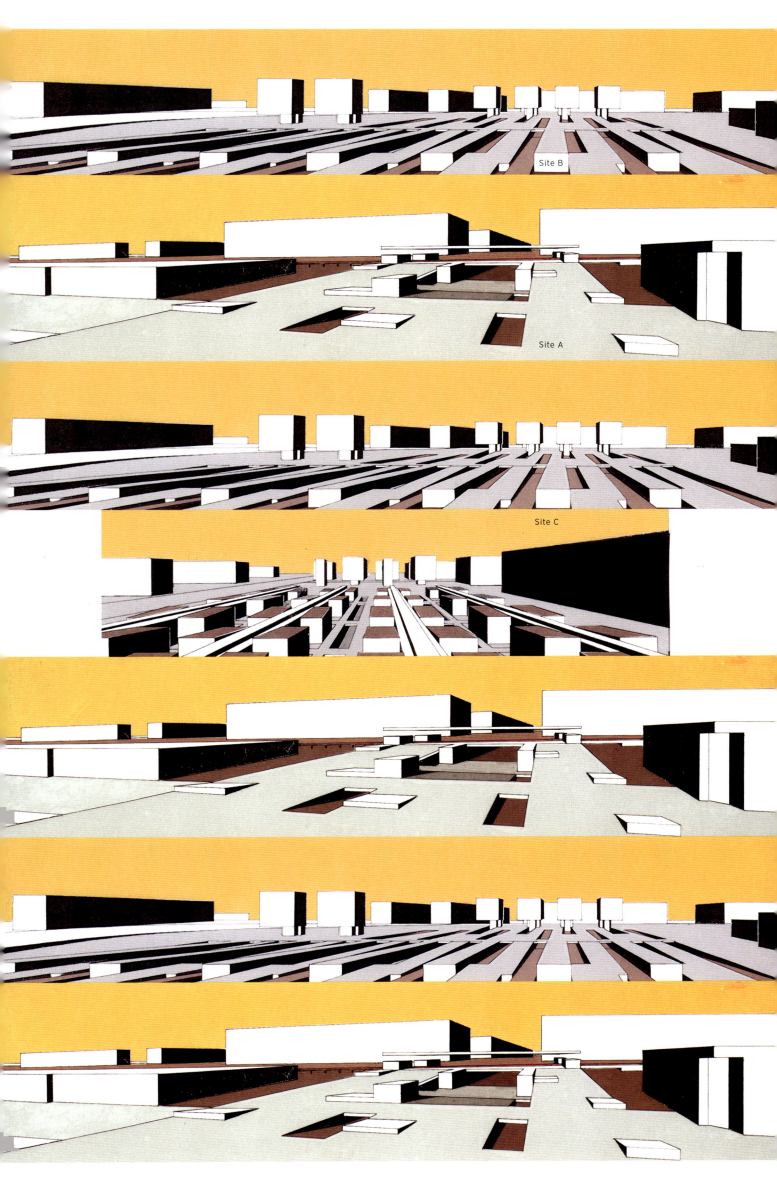

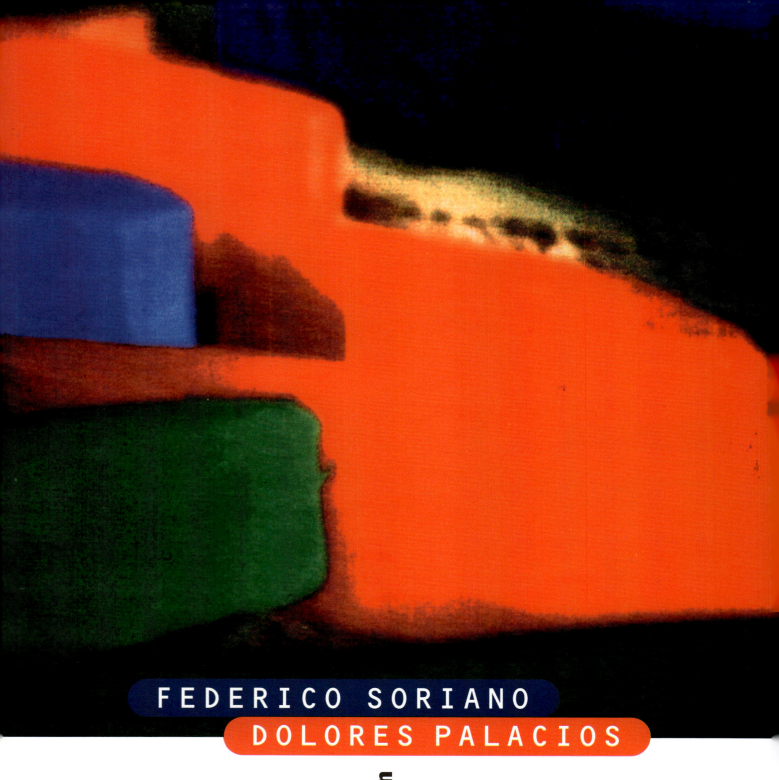

FEDERICO SORIANO
DOLORES PALACIOS

Urban plan

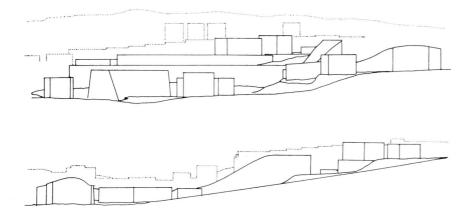

Elevations. General layout

Mina del Morro is set on a sharply sloping site. The approved partial plan somehow attempts to tame and limit the site to a characteristic city outline, making it correspond with the necessary strategies.
We had to make our approach a very different one, more relaxed than preconceived types, innovative, non-urbanistic.
The area of activity should point up its lines and natural rules, and correspond with methods ands aspects existing implicitly on the site. Rather than seeking out regulatory lines or introducing blocks from the extension or the outskirts, what we wanted to do was to bring out the forms lying beneath ground level.
We have brought to light the veins and strata of minerals we are so used to seeing as we drive along motorways between hilly outcrops or see an opencast mine: interpolated strata, colors and textures of different materials.
Our project plays with different blocks which remind us, both in their planimetric configuration and the urban perspectives they produce, of these stratigraphic sections. Their forms are superposed in a perspective, non-axial urban space. Each one will have the colors and texture of several minerals; their stratigraphic composition will even suggest how to effect and order openings, the quartering and joints of the plastering and the cladding of the facade...
The buildings will be low and medium rise, with a will to minimization, loss of scale in the whole, coincidentally point up the green carpet that is to cover all the free surface. The terrain will conserve its topography, because it will be the buildings which adapt to it.
We consequently understand that the city is built of very varying fragments, models and housing units, without lapsing into chaos; it plays on collisions or follows the poetics of the incomplete.
The fabric we propose is a patchwork, a piece of felt impressed with a selection of what the city has to offer.

The final layout as a result of spreading out and folding a cloth

Urban design is dead, according to some writers. Plans and urban developments are being homogenized. In comparison with the lively discussions produced by the modern movement, we find ourselves at a moment when the modern double block, forming a false extension block, has vanquished. So urban design as such declares itself finished. The only city we think or believe we can master is the one which this type produces. Reflection of public space has been reduced to 19th-century models.
As regards house interiors, the law determined what was necessary and fitting some time ago. Today, we no longer know what more there is to a flat —free-priced, luxury or public— than the price or the odd square metre. Yet the cities which grow alone are trying out new models and means of organization, as they always have done.

We ought to think again.
We ought to propose new social models. We ought to take another chance.
TYPES Several housing models came into play here on a larger scale, though many more were worked with in the general plan. In each one, the aim was to plan a home around a private and the exclusive outdoor space.
These are not homes with courtyards in the classical sense, because neither circulation nor configuration are based around the courtyard. Here it is treated as just another part—but an outdoor one, laid out as an extension of the bedrooms as well as the lounge. It provides space for extension without actually being a room. A classification of four types has been established depending on whether they are duplexes or one-story, twoor three bedroom, within 10 or 20 meter spans.

▶ Location BILBAO (SPAIN)
Architects FEDERICO SORIANO, DOLORES PALACIOS
Collaborator CARLOS ARROYO
Project 1996

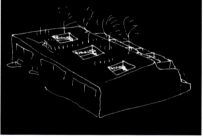

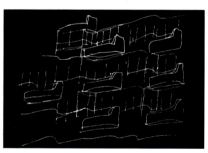

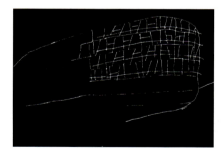

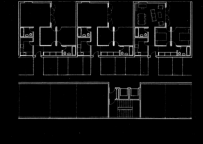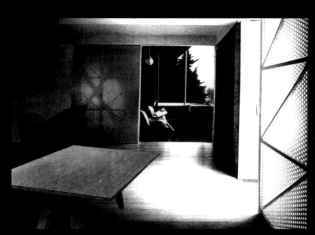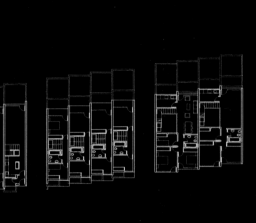

UNITS
BASIC/COMPLEX

FLORIAN RIEGLER
ROGER RIEWE

Housing block

Location
GRAZ (AUSTRIA)
Architect
FLORIAN RIEGLER, ROGER RIEWE
Collaborators
M. MÜLLER, B. THEISSL
Design 1991
Construction 1994
Photographs
M. SPILUTTINI, P. OTT

In an urban environment, balconies and galleries constitute an important element due to the lack of green zones; in rural areas, the absence of these elements is offset by gardens and terraces. This housing block is in an intermediate zone on the urban periphery. Consequently, the balconies here have been disguised à la française, the doors turning 180° towards the interior and, thanks to the small number of floors, one gets the sensation of sitting in the green zone below. In the block there are two types of dwelling: the 50 m² dwellings have 2 1/2 rooms; the 78 m² dwellings have 4 1/2 rooms. This 1/2-room is the result of our desire to design homes with great flexibility of use. (This, however, should not be confused with flexible distribution.) A decisive element in these dwellings is the area of defined use, the extension of which can be increased or reduced in favor of, or in detriment, to the areas of non-defined use. The areas of non-defined use permit the superimposition of a wide variety of uses. The dwellings can be inhabited east to west or north to south. The single bedroom can be converted into a pantry, study, child's bedroom, extension to the living room, etc. The structure of the building consists of reinforced concrete slabs and walls. In the concrete walls, thanks to the skillful joining of the structural elements, it has been possible to reduce the steel elements to a minimum. The facades are formed from sandwich-type prefabricated elements. On the west side, the sliding sunshades are made of nylon; on the east side of expanded metal mesh. All the dwellings are equipped with floor heating.

1. East elevation
2. General floor plan
3. West elevation
4. Plan of dwellings of 2 1/2 and 4 1/2 rooms
5. Interior view with the middle services' strip
6. Section through underground garage

1

2

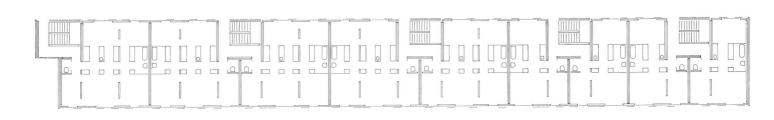

3

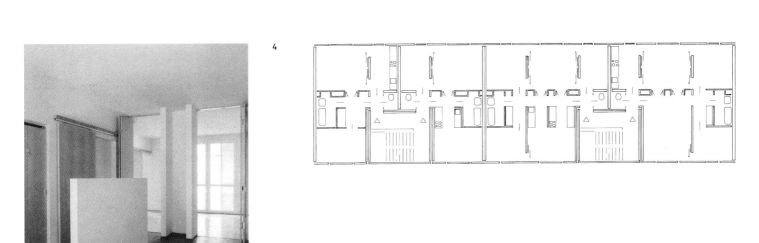

4

5

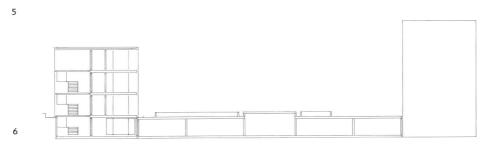

6

157

KEES CHRISTIAANSE

Housing block

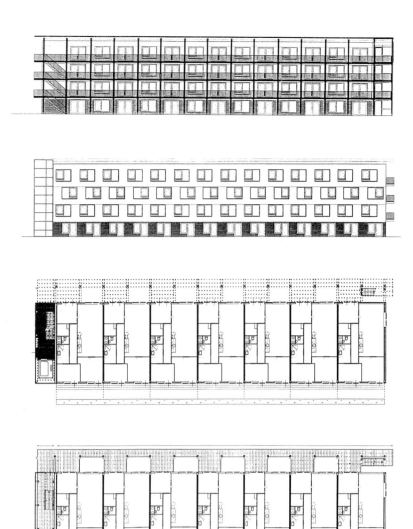

The project is part of a rigorous form of revitalization of a post-war housing area, whereby the existing buildings in the Koekoekstraat and Spreeuwenstraat are being demolished and replaced by new ones. A total of 74 old apartments will be replaced by 100 three-room flats of 75m² in the social housing category. A low budget and demands for same-level entrances necessarily lead to a design with gallery entrances. Because of the many disadvantages this typology involves—a lack of privacy because of the gallery running adjacent to the apartments, less light coming in and the problem of anonymity—a new type of gallery building has been developed.
The gallery is detached from the facade and widened, thus forming a residential thoroughfare at a distance of 3 meters from the building. The apartments' outside terraces are like bridges between the gallery and the building. It is a differentiated, semi-collective space that stimulates contact between the inhabitants. The multistaged transition from collective to private continues in the floor plans of the apartments. The entry consists of French windows, behind which there is a room-size hall instead of a corridor. This hall can be used for a variety of functions.

1. West elevation
2. East elevation
3. Ground floor plan
4. Gallery plan
5. Location. On the left, the block on Koekoekstraat

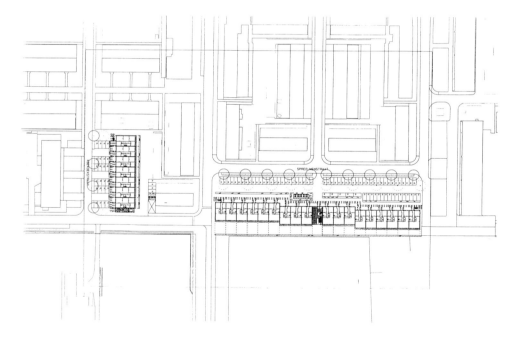

Location AMERSFOORT (NETHERLANDS) – Architect KEES CHRISTIAANSE – Collaborators IRMA VAN OORT, RUUD RIETHOVEN, HILTJE HUIZINGA, ANDRÉ VAN ROSMALEN, EVERT KOLPA, BRANIMIR MEDIC, ERIC SLOTBOOM (Architects) Contractor VASTBOUW, RIJSSEN – Project 1994 – Construction 1997 – Photographs GER VAN DER VLUGT

Views of the semi-communal spaces at the galleries

WILLEM JAN NEUTELINGS

Semi-detached houses

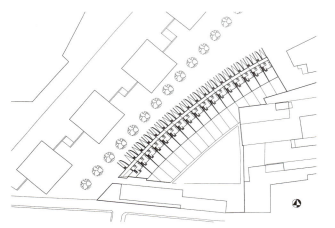

The project is part of an urban development plan designed by the architects Benthem & Crouwel for the 'Thomas de Beer' triangle in Tilburg. It is a block of 17 semi-detached family units which follows the outline envisaged by creating a slightly curved built volume. The dwellings are set out on three levels:
− A basement which is set partially underground with garage and spacious utility room.
− A ground floor with access from the street (a kitchen-dining room at the entrance and a dining room on a raised level on the garden side).
− An upper floor with three bedrooms and a terrace at the front; this level is located under a sloping transversal roof, the repetition of which forms a sawtooth structure.
The two dwellings located at the ends are different.
An extra floor with bedrooms has been added to the northern dwelling, and a larger terrace and basement has been added to the southern one.
Access to the dwellings is gained via a small stairway which bridges the slope leading to the raised walkway and features a series of private terraces at its base.
The base course and basement have been created in ridged concrete, whereas the ground floor is conceived as a staccato of varnished Oregon pine.
The sloping roofs made of streamlined aluminium panels, appear over this wooden strip.

Elevations

Location TILBURG (NETHERLANDS) – Architect WILLEM JAN NEUTELINGS, BV BUREAU VOOR BOUWKUNDE FACILITAIR BEDRIJF (Associate architects) – Collaborators JAGO VAN BERGEN, WILLEM BRUIJN – Contractor SNELLEN MEULEMANSEN VAN SCHAIK BV Project 1993 – Construction 1996 – Photographs JORDI BERNADÓ, RAMON PRAT

1

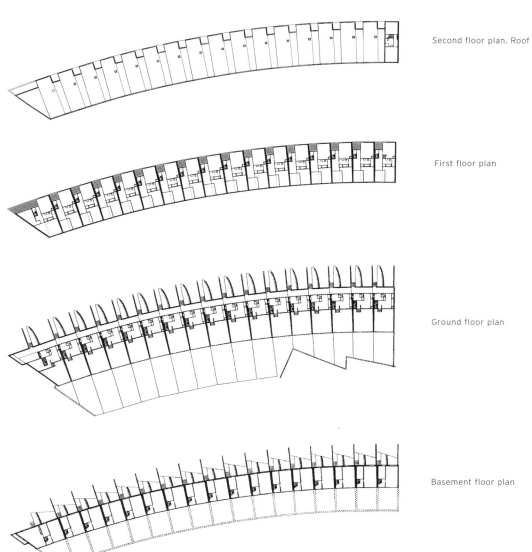

Second floor plan. Roof

First floor plan

Ground floor plan

Basement floor plan

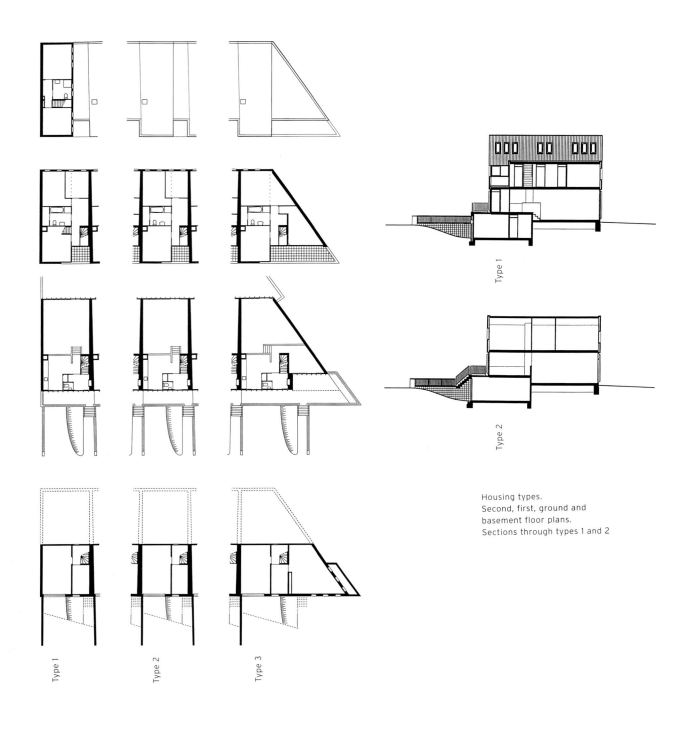

Housing types.
Second, first, ground and basement floor plans.
Sections through types 1 and 2

KAS OOSTERHUIS

Dike housing

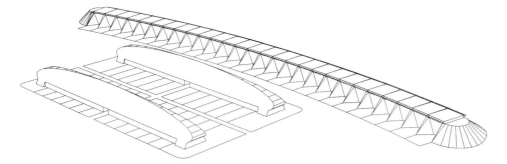

'DIKE HOMES' ZONLAND
Zonland is a new neighborhood in Groningen with an ecological flavour. The project developers could earn bonus points and money by meeting standard ecological criteria. In these two projects: Dijken and Daken; the idea is to emphasize one single criterion and push it to its limits, instead of fitting it nicely into the obvious solution.

DIJKEN (DIKES)

All 29 houses are merged into the volume of a single gently curving artificial dike 200m long. Each house is entered between two reinforced clay triangles rising from the dike. These divide up the lots, enlarging the feeling of individual privacy. On the north side the private terraces are embedded in the sloping sides of the dike, the inhabitants occupying the places resembling dune hollows at the beach. The living rooms are situated on the first floor, offering a wide-angled panorama view north to the open landscape. The bedrooms at ground floor level are cool in summer and comfortably warm during winter due to the mass of the earth.

The clay triangles level out the extremes in temperature, stabilizing at between 6-12° C. They also function as acoustic buffers, greatly contributing to the sense of privacy. Florafilter are constructed along the entire north and south rim of the roof.

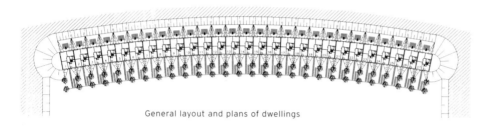

General layout and plans of dwellings

DAKEN (ROOFS)

2 blocks of 14 subsidized owner-occupied dwellings sharing an anthracite-colored tiled roof. A total form which expressly preceded the development of the dwellings. It has finally become a flowing connection of one isosceles triangle between two truncated triangles. The form was remolded and reconsidered until the program could be fitted inside it. The shape is made by the Boolean intersection of two volumes: a stretched triangular bar in one direction, a flattened ellipsoid in the other. The resulting giant pitched roof embraces all fourteen houses in the block in one gentle gesture.

Floor plans and cross section

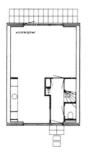  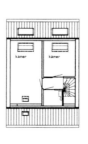 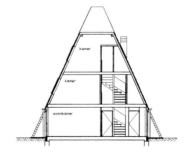

Emplazamiento GRONINGEN (PAÍSES BAJOS) – Arquitecto KAS OOSTERHUIS – Colaboradores JEROEN HUIJSINGA (arquitecto) – Constructora BOUWGROEP HEIJMANS KOOPS – Proyecto 1994 – Ejecución 1995

WILLEM JAN NEUTELINGS

Kustzone 4e Kwadrant

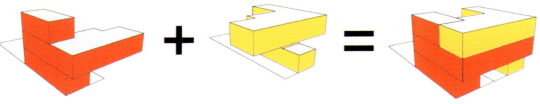

Housing units.
A 6m-wide terraced house converted into a 12m-wide 'panorama house'

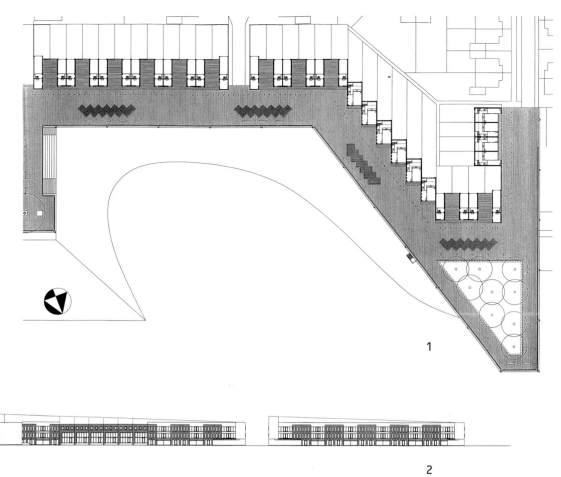
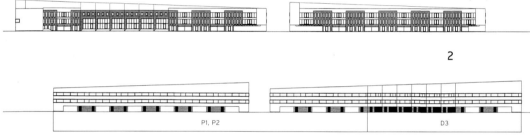
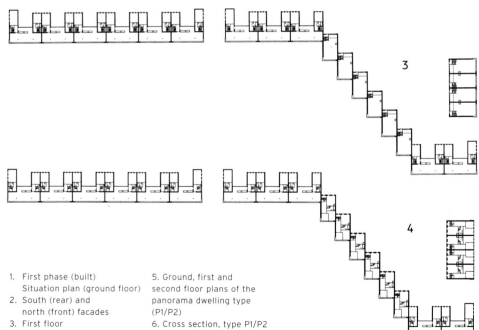

Location HUIZEN (NETHERLANDS) – Architects NEUTELINGS RIEDIJK ARCHITECTEN BV, WILLEM JAN NEUTELINGS, MICHIEL RIEDIJK, WILLEM BRUIJN, GERRIT SCHILDER – Technical design BUREAU BOUWKUNDE ROTTERDAM Structure INGENIEURSGROEP VAN ROSSUM, AMSTERDAM – Contractor COEN HAGEDOORN BOUW BV, HUIZEN Landscaping JUURLINK & GELUK, ROTTERDAM – Project 1994 – Construction 1996 – Photographs R. PRAT, J. BERNADÓ

1. First phase (built) Situation plan (ground floor)
2. South (rear) and north (front) facades
3. First floor
4. Second floor
5. Ground, first and second floor plans of the panorama dwelling type (P1/P2)
6. Cross section, type P1/P2
7. Cross section, type D3

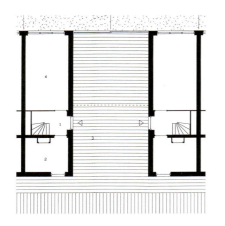
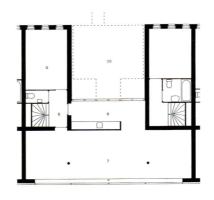
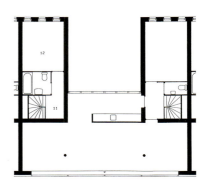

5

Fulfilling a strategic role in the local property market, the scheme sought to achieve a balance between utilizing the environmental conditions of the place and a beneficial quality-price ratio. In order to achieve a specific 'local atmosphere' it is necessary to boost the intrinsic qualities of Huizen, a coastal town on Lake Gooimeer, through the internal distribution of the dwellings and their prime orientations.

The types of dwelling are mainly designed for families whose children are in the process of leaving the family nucleus. Equal importance is given to questions of safety, comfort, privacy or the quality and dimensions of the external spaces.
The plan, which creates a frontal part overlooking the lake, is set out in three parts:
1. Dike buildings (buildings with views). Frontal sections of varying height form a main facade overlooking Lake Gooimeer.
The lengthways setting out of these frontal sections –spanning 12 m– affords expansive views of the Gooimeer. The back of the building, which is south-facing, contains the bedrooms and a terrace which allows light to enter through the kitchen between both facades.
2. Coastline: public space like a coastline and part of the boulevard which leads to the center of Huizen.

3. Marshland buildings (Dwellings-Gooimeer): five one-off blocks located in a prominent position between land and sea. Each block comprises thirteen dwellings and these are set out in accordance with the particular conditions of their site and orientation on the water. Pedestrian and vehicular access are gained via a roadway which floats on the reed-beds and links the promenade to these residential blocks on the water.

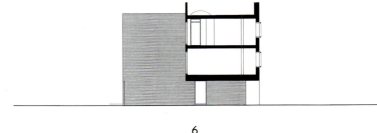

6

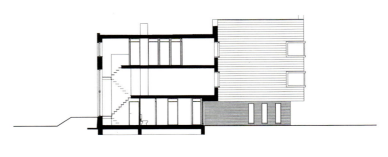

7

JOSEP LLUÍS MATEO

Housing complex

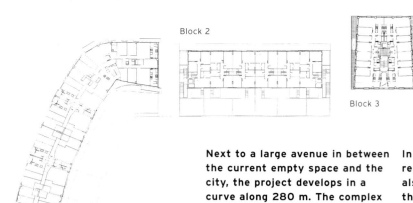

Block 2

Block 3

Next to a large avenue in between the current empty space and the city, the project develops in a curve along 280 m. The complex is defined as a long building and two small constructions at the edge which allow the viewer to understand the scale and the unitary dimensions of the large linear block. The main building is divided into two bodies: a wide base, partly buried, onto which a narrower body containing the houses slides. The treatment of surfaces increases this intensity: in the convex part, the base made of galvanized steel and glass supports a band of red bricks and systematically organized perforations. An irregular pattern of small yellow bricks emphasizes those spaces chose as being special (end/beginning-lessened concavities-general passage).

In front of this external flat and reiterative vision, the convex part also expresses standardization throughout large pieces of artificial stone (3 x 1,5 m) with black bands at the thresholds, narrow lines of glass and different wrinkled textures in white. It is intended to dematerialize the concrete panelling and, paradoxically, to transform it into something close to textile, and on a domestic scale adequate to the living rooms it encloses. The glass surfaces of the enclosures and balconies appear at different levels. The two small buildings at the edge complete the whole: the first one (composed by larger, duplex-type apartments) giving a sense of continuity to the base; the second appearing as a final banner.

Block 1

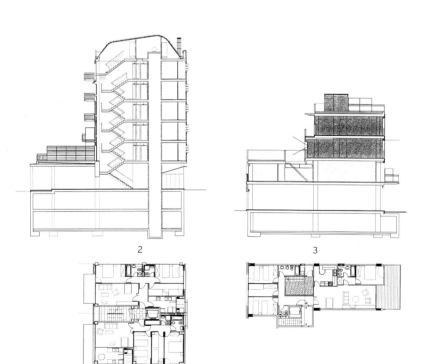

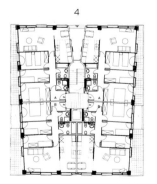

1. General layout of blocks Block 1, block 2, block 3
2. Block 1. Cross section and corner type dwelling
3. Block 2. Cross section and main floor plan
4. Block 3. Floor plan typology

Location TERRASSA (SPAIN) – Architect JOSÉ LUIS MATEO – Contractor PARC OLÍMPIC EGARA, GRUP NOVAFORMA, SA
Surveyor LLUÍS CREUS, EMILI SÁNCHEZ – Project 1993 **(Competition, first prize)** – Construction 1994-1999 – Photographs JORDI MIRALLES

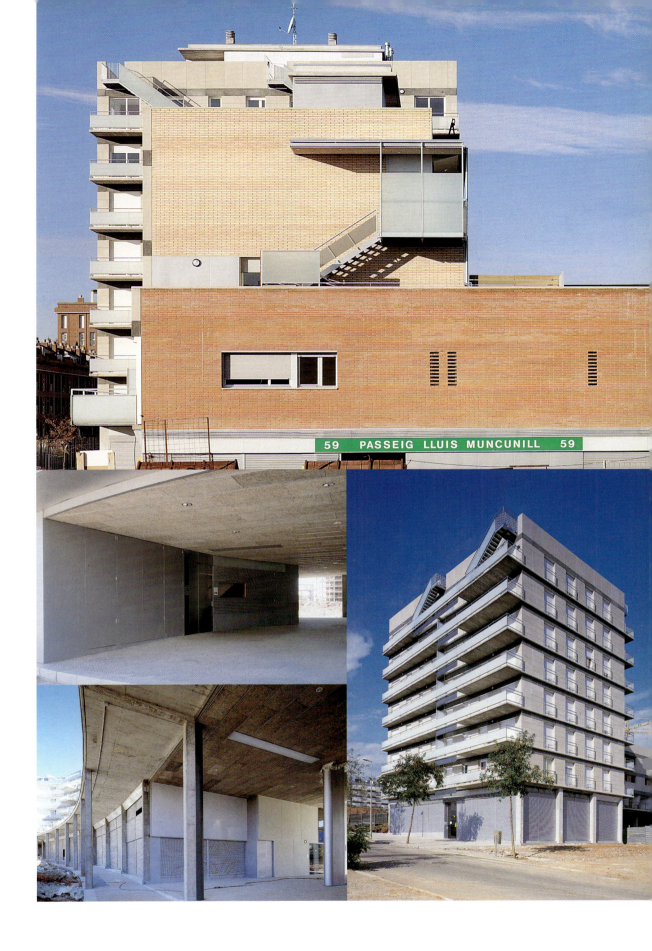

HANS KOLLHOFF

Residential building

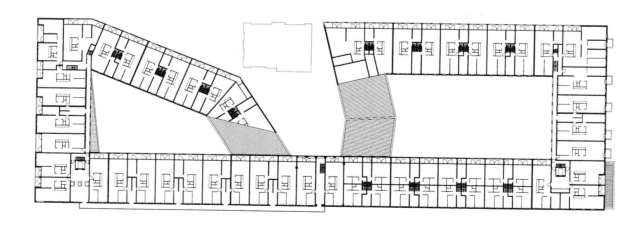

184

Location AMSTERDAM – Architects HANS KOLLHOFF, CHRISTIAN RAPP
Collaborators ARNO VAN DER MARK (Artist), BOUWADVIESBUREAU HEIJKMANN (Structure)
Project 1989 – Construction 1994 – Photographs RAMON PRAT, JORDI BERNADÓ

Seldom does an architect in a Western city have the opportunity to put ideas into practice without coming up against any form of resistance. The structures within which political decisions are made and the committees which adopt the role of client are set on compromise. The only possibility left open to the architect is to assume the task of documenting events and to accept that conflict needs to be incorporated in the building. The architect has to produce a mass of constellations which are apparently arbitrary and contradictory, and, with these, make a solid and coherent whole. Furthermore, the architect also has to face the problem stemming from the fact that, at present, buildings are expected to be infinitely adaptable and interchangeable, and they are therefore deprived of their regional context.

Under economic pressure to create something optimal in every aspect, everything becomes nothing more than a shoe box which the architect decorates as best he thinks fit. Current building schemes challenge formal analogies in such a way that, if the architect does not wish to sell himself as a window-dresser, he is obliged to examine in depth, and find vestiges of, formal intensity even in the most commonplace schemes and projects.

In Amsterdam we have a master plan which is more or less defined. The motive behind it is the intensity of large, discrete buildings facing the sea in an area of old warehouses.

Gradually, the initially proposed form for the 170 x 60 meter block underwent a morphological transformation. The intention of providing the side of the building with natural light and a good view ended up with the side-wing having to be moved back. Respecting the wishes of future residents to preserve what remained of the park in the old warehouse district, the block was opened out on the first four floors of the most prominent side. Finally, it was necessary to find a solution to the contradiction between the building in the courtyard and a place facing the sea: the external wall of the block which faced the sea was moved back in order to let the sunlight coming from the south into the courtyard, and to give the residents in the flats facing the courtyard a sea view. Later, it was necessary to make a wedge-shaped incision at another corner of the block in order to create a narrow street between the new block and the neighbouring building. The obligation to provide a range of small flats of different types made it necessary to change the form of the taller flats: access galleries, with protruding glass panels which were placed along the side of the northern external wall whereas, on the other side, two galleries, two stories high, were set into the volume of the building.

Natural materials –pressed brick, fired on an open flame– and the painstaking work of the specialists gave this unfamiliar, huge form a homely touch.

WIEL ARETS

Apartment tower

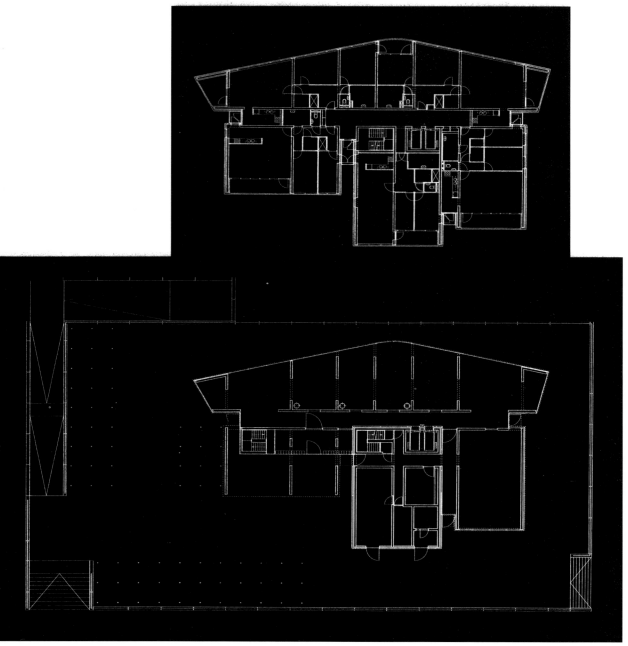

Ground floor and basic floor plan of apartments

The design consists of four elements: four separate yet closely-grouped towers. The whole has twenty-one stories. Each story —each level of housing— contains five apartments. There are five penthouses on the roof. The tower block stands on the island formerly occupied by the Royal Netherlands Steamboat Company, with a view of Amsterdam in one direction and the waters of Ijsselmeer in the other. The four elements comprising the tower block confront the ground plane at different heights. Fluctuating in height with regard to the ground floor level, the four elements are so designed as to create a skyline, as it were, at ground floor level. There is also a view through the indoor car park from this level.

Location AMSTERDAM — Architect WIEL ARETS — Collaborators ELMAR KLEUTERS, PAUL KUITENBROUWER, RENÉ THIJSSEN (Project architects), ANCA ARENZ, IVO DANIËLS, JO JANSSEN, MAURICE PAULUSSEN, HENRIK VUUST (Assistants), Buro van Eck (Structure), T & H BV ADVIESBURO INSTALLATIETECHNIEK (Mechanical engineering), WILMA BOUW (Contractor) — Project 1993 — Construction 1995 — Photographs RAMON PRAT, JORDI BERNADÓ

191

PHILIPPE GAZEAU

Housing block

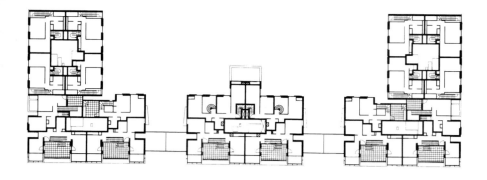

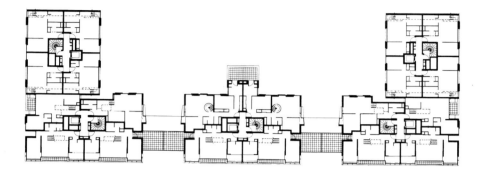

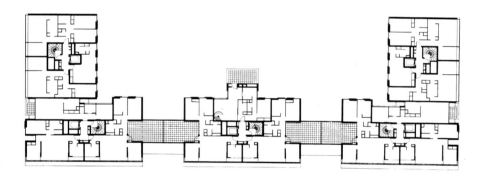

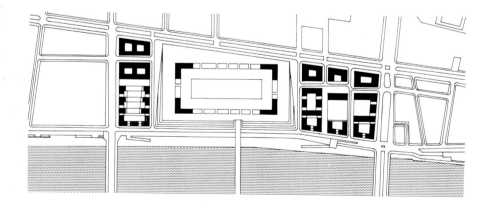

A PLANE, A FACADE

The facade overlooking the embankment displays the panoramic bias which is the result of the internal layout of the apartments and the strong relation established between the living areas and the river. There are views over the Seine for the first three levels above the floor, which is set back, through wide horizontal strips, projecting from the main body while respecting the prescribed alignment. This determination to create a panorama is reinforced inside by a strip in the form of a false ceiling and wooden parquet, pontoon-style, creating a promenade along the facade and joining the living spaces together. The horizontal treatment of the facade thus reflects this panoramic relationship between the apartments and the embankment and the river. These strips, centering the view of the Seine from the apartments, are far from mere balconies or terraces. This type of use, which generally sits uncomfortably with street or embankment, is correctly applied here in the case of these garden terraces, sheltered in the indentations or on terraces which give onto the inner garden. These elements serve as an outdoor sunscreen, as casing for outside blinds or indoor shutters, and as a receptacle for storing heating apparatus. The top two duplex levels indicate these apartments' singular situation between river and sky in a typology deriving from villa-type buildings, adapting easily to the repetitive system of the three adjacent blocks. The glazed, double-height volumes, protected by brise-soleils in iroko wood, and the terraces interconnected by interior or exterior stairways reflect the vertical organization of these apartments. Each duplex has direct access to the roof terrace, which is fitted out and covered (like the garden terraces of the indentations) with wooden slabs.

1. Top duplex level 2
2. Top duplex level 1
3. Floor plan typology
4. Site plan. The housing developments on either side of the Grande Bibliothèque of Bercy

Location PARIS — Architect PHILIPPE GAZEAU — Collaborators AGNÈS CANTIN, JACQUES FORTE. GET INGENIERIE (Quantity surveyors) — Contractor LES MAÇONS PARISIENS — Project 1996 Construction 1997 — Photographs JEAN-MARIE MONTHIERS, RAMON PRAT, JORDI BERNADÓ

The facades giving onto Rues de Tolbiac and Domrémy
join the gabled facade of
the abutment on the embankment side with a second part
which comprises the street-side of the building.
The facade of this building offers the maximum in views
and light to the living area of the apartments, which all run diagonally, with the lounge overlooking the street
and the bedroom overlooking the garden, while the studio gives onto the garden.
The street facade picks up the idea of a difference in treatment and volume between the lower levels and the duplex of the top two levels, but by taking the latter as artists' studios rather than villa-type buildings.
The volumes and facades overlooking the garden and the interior of the block are very different to those giving onto the street and embankment.
Sliding shutters in front
of the windows giving onto the garden, sheltered from the commotion of the embankment, go to make up the main
elements of the outer skin.

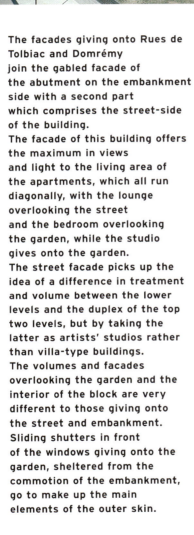

FRANCIS SOLER

Apartment building

SERIES WITHOUT END

Our first task was to create a series of stages, freed from the constraints of habitual structure, onto which we projected, as onto a screen, a kind of strange, singular, modern theatre in which the acts of a play would be simultaneously played out without ever disclosing the end.

We provided the tenants with the practical means for their lifestyles and forms of expression, allowing the individuals to organize their days and nights in the comfortable apartments they were given, in the knowledge that they could fit them out as they pleased. We had been careful to stratify all the available space along the street to create a kind of 'millefeuille' in light cement, underpinned only by a longitudinal wall and a series of columns in the facade.

We regrouped different-sized apartments around one lift, as we considered this to be good for the building's community life.

The apartments all received plenty of sunlight and had several views; all had a large living room, at least one large bedroom and, above all, a proper kitchen. Looking, the sun, day and night thus came into play like so many candidates for a scenario writer, and the vertical layers we proposed to the tenant, in their multiple combinations, functioned as answers to the questions asked.

The first layer, the most intimate and innermost, showed a strange resemblance to a photographic gelatine printed with figurative scenes taken from early painting. Candelabra, standard lamps, lights and the glow of televisions would light up these gelatines from inside, like a myriad boxes of lights bringing out the tones of their chromatic ranges.

The second, stricter layer coming straight after the gelatines was nothing other than a banal succession of glass panels, perfectly transparent from floor to ceiling. Its purpose was a simple one. First of all, it had merely to provide the tenants with the climatic limit to their apartments, at the same time giving as much light as possible and the widest possible views. And then disappear. The unpredictable, uncontrollable effects of reflections on the glass were to put the finishing touches to the work.

The third, lightest and outermost layer first places a restraint on the sun and the eyes of the curious, and also fulfills one of our recent dreams, which was to create the illusion that a building, entirely shrouded in fabric, could demystify the legendary massiveness attached to architecture.

This could be a rational development of the idea of

contributing a light touch to the alignment of the street by giving the project a certain immateriality. We protected the homeliest spaces in the apartments and their extended balconies from the sun.

This is perhaps not a building in the traditional sense of the word, but rather a contemporary work which transposes into the real world a kind of accumulation of images in perpetual motion which bear witness, in time, to the importance of certain abstract, ephemeral forms of architecture in the construction of our cities, on the threshold of the twenty-first century.

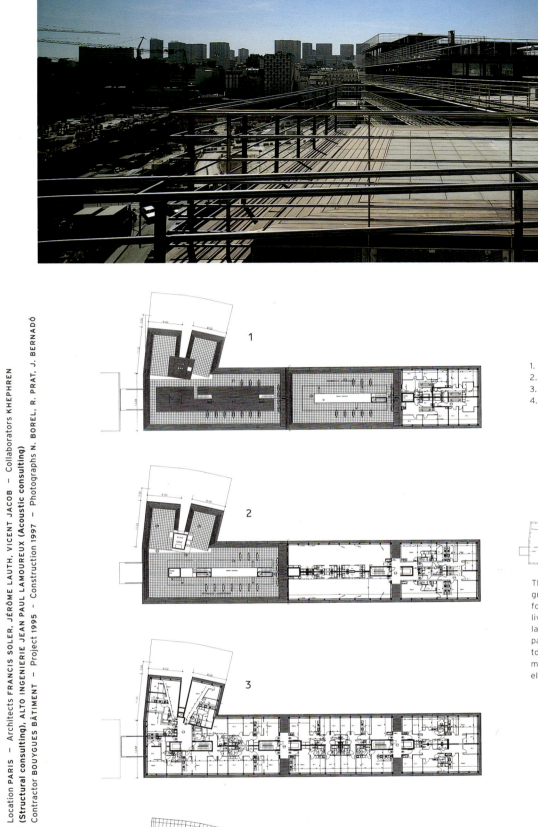

Location PARIS – Architects FRANCIS SOLER, JÉRÔME LAUTH, VICENT JACOB – Collaborators KHEPHREN (Structural consulting), ALTO INGENIERIE JEAN PAUL LAMOUREUX (Acoustic consulting) Contractor BOUYGUES BÂTIMENT – Project 1995 – Construction 1997 – Photographs N. BOREL, R. PRAT, J. BERNADÓ

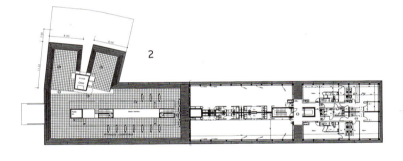

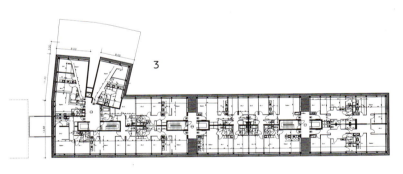

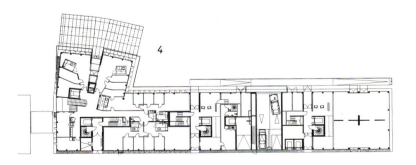

1. Ninth floor plan
2. Eighth floor plan
3. Typical floor plan
4. Ground floor plan

The project originally offered great freedom and versatility for the occupation of the living spaces. A modulated layout with no previous partitions left future occupants to choose the number of spatial modules and the facade elements for each apartment.

motif A1   motif A2   motif D1   motif D2   motif C1   motif C2

motif E1   motif E2   motif F1   motif F2   motif G1   motif G2

HOLL OOSTERHUIS NEUTELINGS MVRDV

HYBRID
ENTITIES

STEVEN HOLL

Makuhari housing

205

IDEA: Lightness = activity = sound; Heaviness = reinforced blocks = silence.
The new town of Makuhari is located on a dredged embankment next to Tokyo Bay.
The town planners have established rules for building with height restrictions, tree-lined streets, shopping areas, etc. Each city block has to be planned by three or four different architects in an attempt to create variety. Our idea puts forward the integration of two types of structure: heavy and silent buildings and light and active buildings.
The silent buildings define the form of the urban spaces and the passageways with small flats which are reached via the courtyards or interior gardens.
The structures with concrete walls have thick facades and a rhythmic repetition of the openings (with variations between windows or surfaces). Gently sloping, according to the arbiter of sunlight, they give a soft curve to the space and passageways and interlink with both movement and the lightweight structures.
The celebration of the miniature and natural phenomena is resumed again by the active, light strength of personalities and individual schemes.
These individualized sounds invade the silence of the reinforced buildings.
Inspired by *The Narrow Path to the Deep North*, by Basho, the semi-public interior gardens and the arrangement in perspective of the active houses make up an inner journey.
The interiors of the silent buildings are designed by Koichi Sone and Toshio Enomoto (Kajima Design).

Site plan

Shadow study

Location CHIBA (JAPAN) – Architects STEVEN HOLL, KAJIMA DESIGN (Associate architects) – Collaborators TOMOAKI TANAKA (Project architect), MARIO GOODEN, THOMAS JENKINSON, JANET CROSS, TERRY SURJAN (Design team), ANDERSON LEE, SUMITO TAKASHINA, SEBASTIAN SCHULZE, GUNDO SOHN, JUSTIN KORHAMMER, BRADFORD KELLEY, LISINA FINGERHUTH, ANNA MULLER, JAN KINSBERGEN (Design development team), HIDEAKI ARIIZUMI (Consultant), MASATO KAWASHIMA (Landscape consultant), HERVÉ DESCOTTES (Lighting consultant), KEIZO MIYAGAWA, KENICHI NISHI (Structural engineering), YOSHIAKI WADA, YASUO OHASHI (Mechanical and electrical engineering) – Project 1992 – Construction 1994-1996 – Photographs PAUL WARCHOL

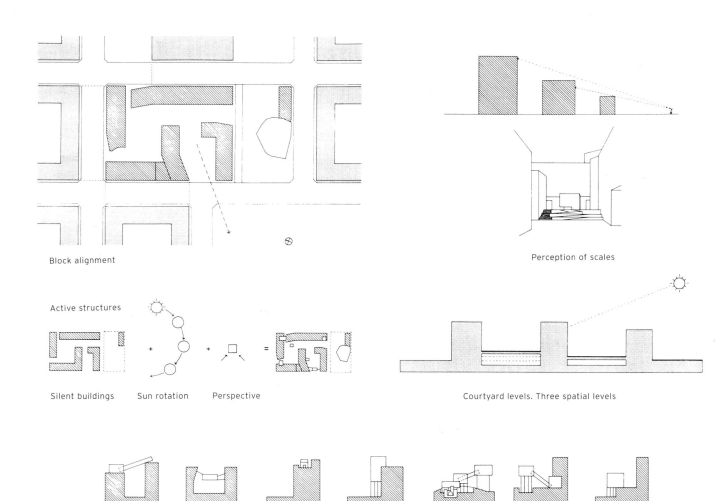

Block alignment

Perception of scales

Active structures

Silent buildings   Sun rotation   Perspective

Courtyard levels. Three spatial levels

Correlational chart. Urban relation: Figure / Ground

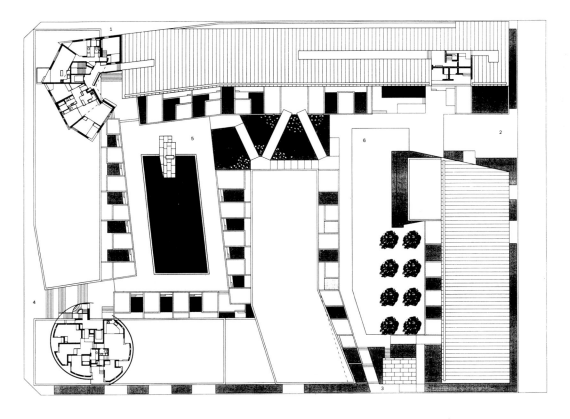

Roof plan
1. East gate
2. South gate
3. West gate
4. North gate
5. North court
6. South court

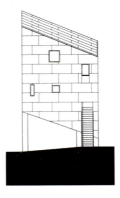
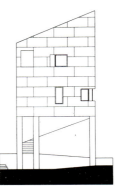

West gate house.
Floor plans, elevations and sections

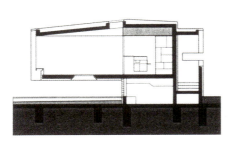
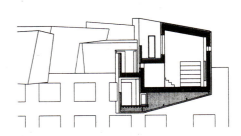

North gate house. Floor plan and section

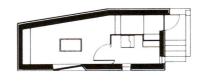

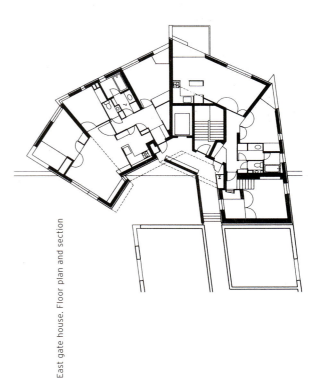

East gate house. Floor plan and section

KAS OOSTERHUIS

Dancing facades

This housing development consists of 34 upmarket, owner-occupied houses divided among three rows. Two rows consist of patio houses with numerous possibilities for infill and extension. They have extra-deep front gardens and no back garden, as the rear of the houses is set on the property boundary.
The units in the third row seem semi-detached, yet are in fact terraced houses. The basic unit is the same in all three rows. The distorted, multicolored roof-structures are attempts to separate the concepts of 'building' and 'housing' and use a spatially rhythmic object to facilitate a different understanding of what is meant by city, urbanism and coherence. This all takes place above the horizon, particularly in those parts of the building that are visible at neighborhood level. The ground floor is, as far as possible, 'absent' and 'ordinary'. A less exposed dwelling lies within the taut rhythm of brick frames, behind which lie hidden patios and sun rooms, places for dustbins, carports, garages and complete dwellings.

What at first sight appear to be three differently elaborated rows of single-family dwellings are in fact linked freestanding and semi-detached dwellings. The ground floor has been treated as an entity: tucked away behind a dark brick facade surface with large, regular openings, are living rooms, entrances, storage areas, garages and patios. Rising above this in stuccoed multi-colored volumes designed by Ilona Lénard, are one- and two-room extensions of the dwellings. Despite this rigorous approach, occupants have been allowed considerable freedom of choice. The patio can be closed on one or two sides, the living space can be extended, a carport or a garage can be added. Another striking feature is that the rear facades of two rows have been placed along the plot boundary so that the back doors open directly onto the municipal green space. The result is very deep front gardens and a much more generous street profile.
The dancing facades free the rows from their automatic housing associations and endow them with a sculptural presence.

Location GRONINGEN (NETHERLANDS) – Architect KAS OOSTERHUIS – Collaborators JEROEN HUIJSINGA (Architect) ILONA LÉNARD (Artist) – Contractor BOUWBEDRIJF SLOKKER – Project 1994 – Construction 1995

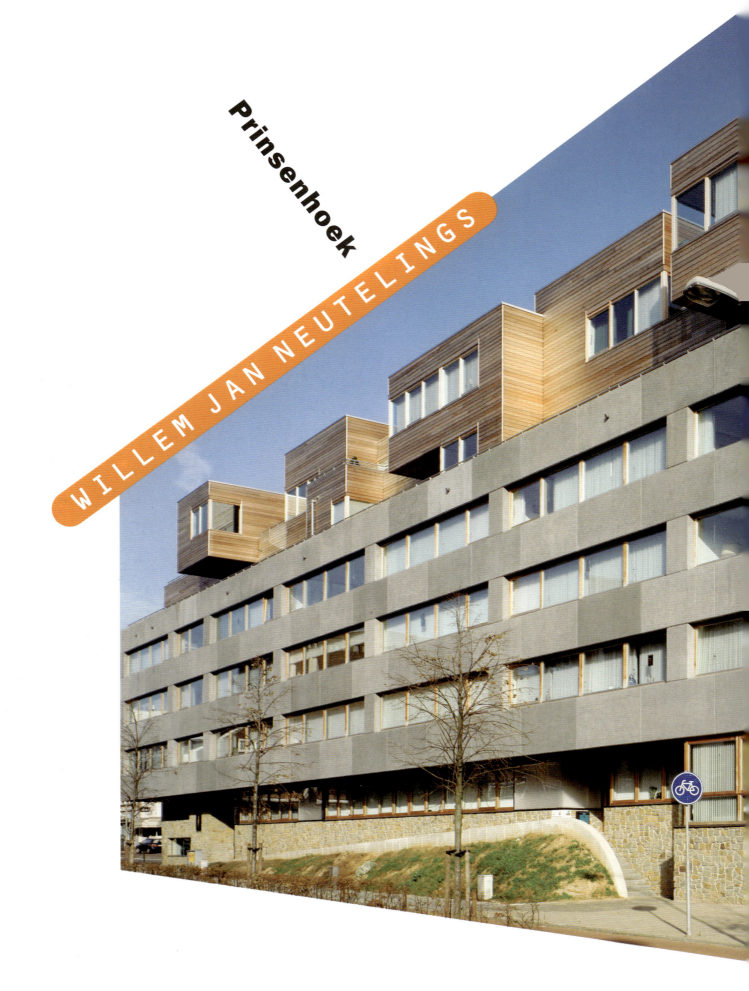

Prinsenhoek

WILLEM JAN NEUTELINGS

The Prinsenhoek project, situated on one of the most important intersections in the center of Sittard, consists of three elements grouped around an inner garden: a 19th-century villa, an apartment block and a car park. The old villa, which would have been demolished under the old city ordinance, has been kept as an attractive historical element in the complex, being remodelled to accommodate. The gardens of the villa are used as a linking element in the project, a quiet oasis in the city. The horizontal man of the new building is designed to lie along the length of the site: a socle of offices and shops, plus a block of twenty-six apartments with an additional six large penthouses above creating an articulated roofscape.
The entrances, bay windows, gates and access routes are finished in robust Ardennes flagstones, forming a socle of urban fabric.
The three middle floors consist of a strong rectangular volume. This volume has a rhythmic sequence of deeply-set windows set in its anthracite-grey concret facade. The line of the roof is defined by the sculptural play of cedar-clad volumes whose cantilevers and setbacks form luxurious terraces from which the occupants can enjoy a panoramic view of Sittard's city center.

Location SITTARD (NETHERLANDS)
Architects WILLEM JAN NEUTELINGS ARCHITECTUUR BV
Collaborators ARCHITEKTENBURO SCHINKEL-BENNING BV
WEST 8 LANDSCAPE ARCHITECTS BV
Consulting
BV BUREAU VOOR BOUWKUNDE
Structural engineering
INGENIEURSBUREAU A. PALTE BV
Main contractor
BOBEMA BOUW- EN BETONMAATSCHAPPIJ BV
Design 1992
Construction 1995
Photographs KIM ZWARTS

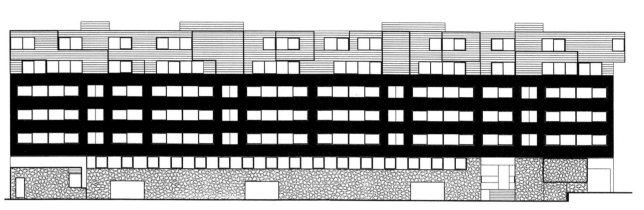

1

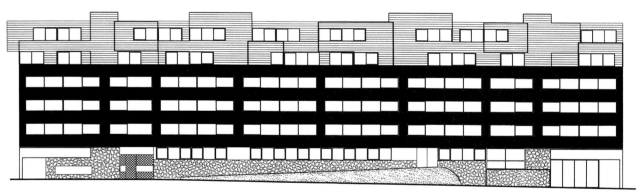

2

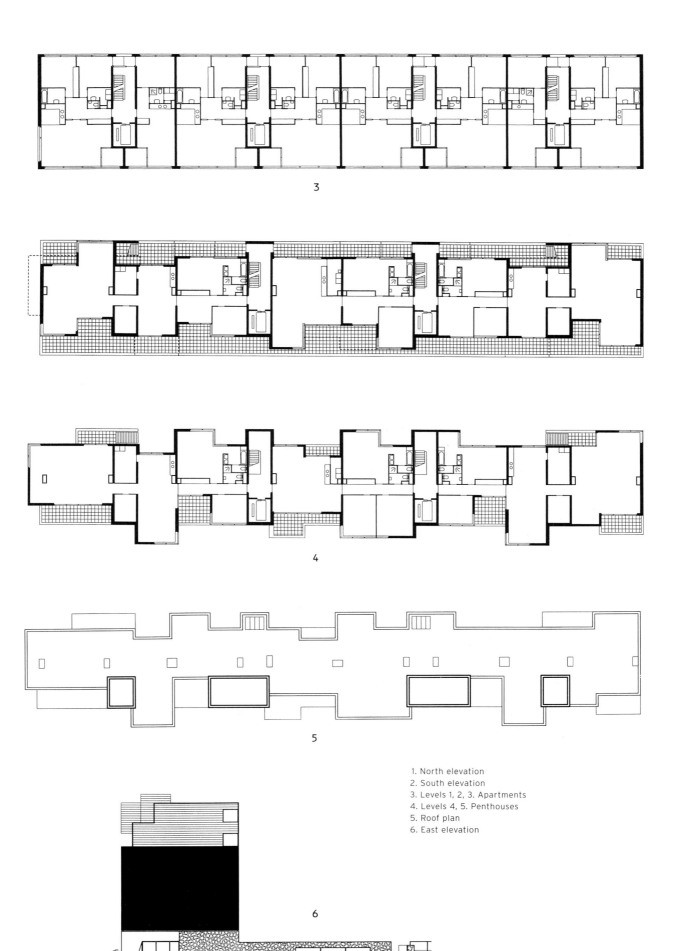

1. North elevation
2. South elevation
3. Levels 1, 2, 3. Apartments
4. Levels 4, 5. Penthouses
5. Roof plan
6. East elevation

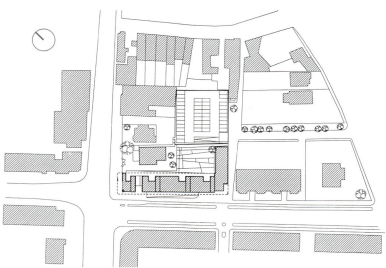

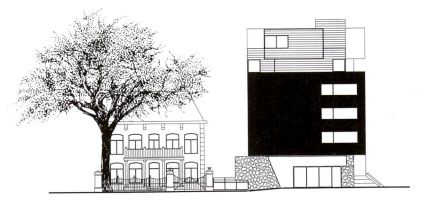

North facade. Entrance to the interior garden.
The existing villa was preserved by integrating it into the project

MVRDV

100 Wozoco's

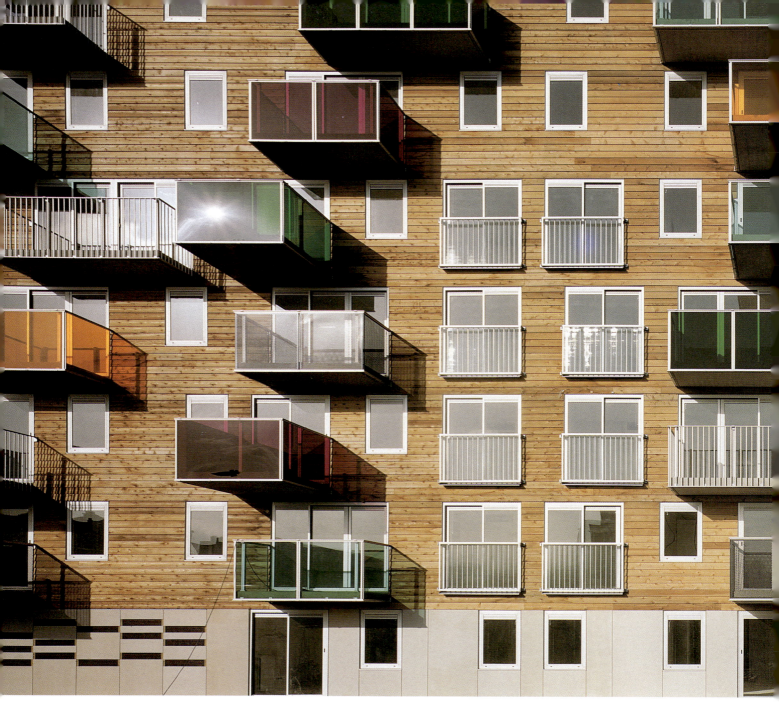

1

1. North facade
2. South facade
3. West and east facades, with elevations of the cantilevered volumes

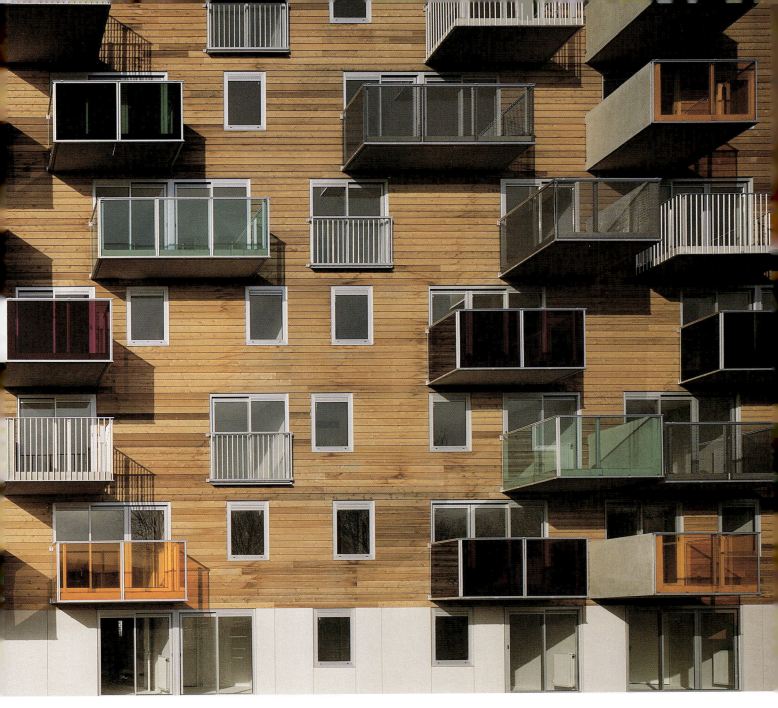

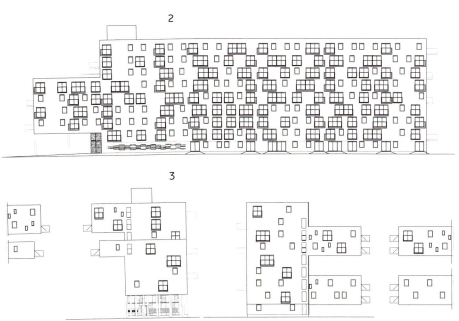

223

HOUSES FOR ELDERLY PEOPLE

Set in the increasingly dense Garden City area of west Amsterdam (Westelijke Tuinsteden), a block of 100 apartments for '55-plussers' had to be placed.
The zonification of the area and the north-south orientation of the building made it impossible to position the 100 apartments in the block; it would only hold 87.
The remaining 13 were cantilevered from the north facade of the block with steel trusses so that each hanging apartment gets sun on an east- or west-facing facade (in Holland it is not viable to build north-facing apartments). In this way the characteristic first floor of such neighborhoods remains as open and green as possible. The prototypical level of density for these areas is predefined.

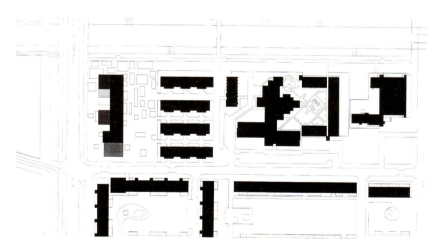

▶ Location AMSTERDAM - Architects WINY MAAS, JACOB VAN RIJS, NATHALIE DE VRIES - Collaborators WILLEM TIMMER, ARJA MULDER, FRANS DE WITTE, DGMR RAADGEVEND INGENIEURS (Structure), JAC BISSCHOPS (Collaborating artist) - Contractor INTERVAM BML, PIETERS BOUW TECHNIEK - Project 1994 - Construction 1997 - Photographs JORDI BERNADÓ, RAMON PRAT

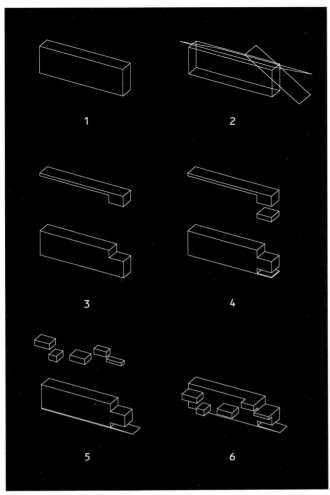

MODIFICATIONS TO THE BUILT VOLUME

To ensure adequate sunlight in the surrounding buildings, only 87 of the 100 units could be realised within the block. If the remaining 13 dwellings were to have been placed elsewhere on the site, the open space would have been further reduced. The solution came by 'cantilevering' them along the north facade. Combining the east-west orientation of the cantilevered units with the north-south orientation of the dwellings inside the block provides a welcome articulation.

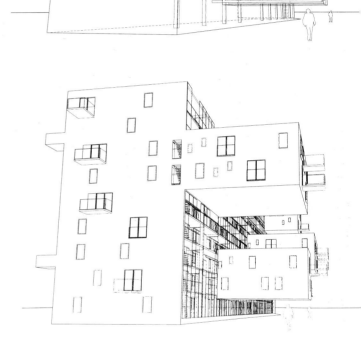

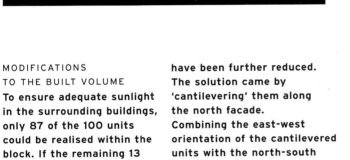

By predetermining the number of inner walls in the basic block type, 7-8% of the cost could be saved, which was enough to compensate for the 50% expense increase on the cantilevered units

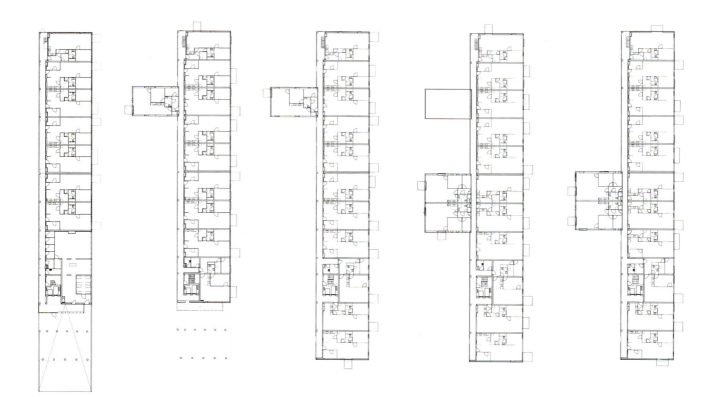

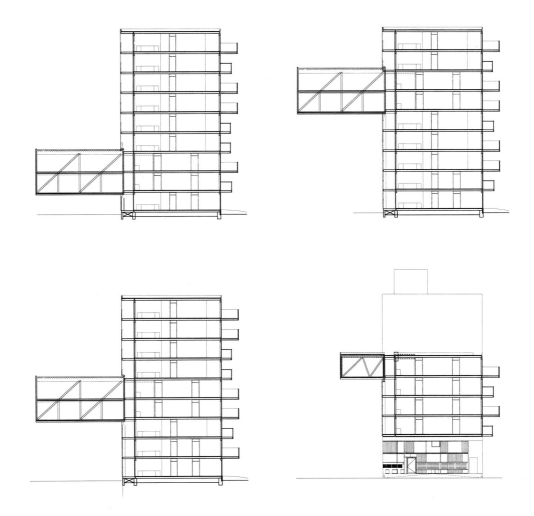

1. Cross sections through cantilevers
2. Floor plans. The spartan gallery flat typology with corridor markedly improves with the changing perspectives on each level

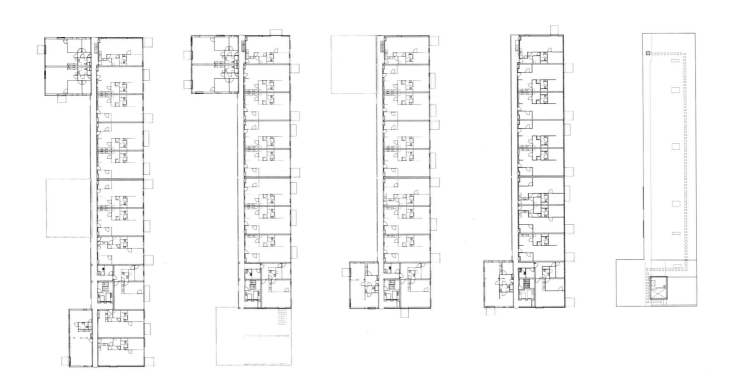

LLINÀS GAZEAU SOLER MARZELLE-MANESCAU-STEEG NOUVEL SOUTO DE MOURA KEIM-SILL

INCISIONS

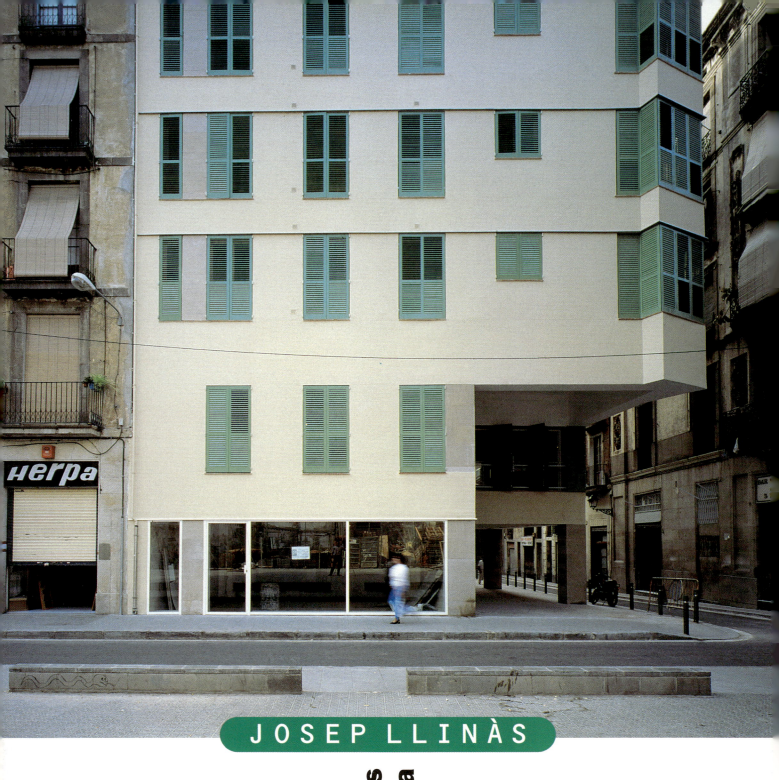

JOSEP LLINÀS

Dwellings in Ciutat Vella

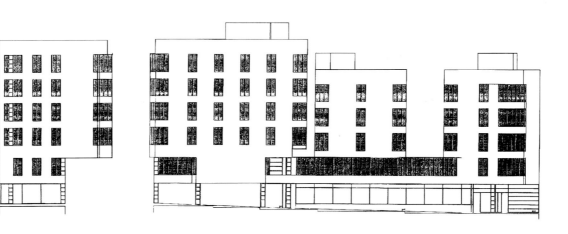

Location BARCELONA – Architect JOSEP LLINÀS – Collaborators E. MONTE, J. VERA (Architects)
J. MARTÍ (Surveyor) – R. BRUFAU (Structure) – Design 1989 – Construction 1994 – Photographs J. BERNADÓ

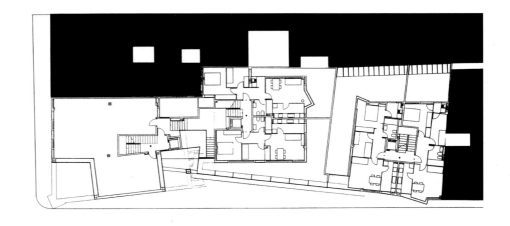

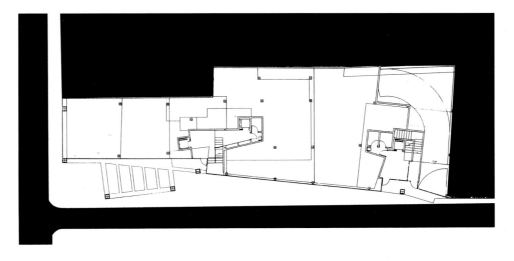

Elevations from C. Carme and C. Roig. Basic, first and ground floor plans

Building in Ciutat Vella should perhaps not be contemplated as a problem of approach to or distance from the stylistic constants of this part of Barcelona. This would be a fundamental consideration in the case, say, of the Eixample[1], where probably the most serious problem an architect would have to face is the definition of the vertical facade which encloses the site between buildings.
The critical situation of Ciutat Vella, overburdened with uses and for too long ignored in terms of urban conservation or refurbishment, calls for reflection on the effect which any project carried out there would produce on public space. If, as I said earlier, in the Eixample the problem might be in the definition of the vertical limit, here attention to horizontal relationships strikes me as far more important: street-buildings; public spaces-domestic spaces; intermediate spaces between the front door of buildings and the road on which traffic circulates.
The conventional line which separates houses from the street, which is becoming the line of confrontation between the individual rights of residents and those of the City Hall is still, in Ciutat Vella, a line without definition, a strip of tolerance and agreement among people on the fringe of the culture of sanction and infraction. To make the street and consolidate this strip was the objective of this project, sited at the confluence between Carrer Carme and Carrer Roig. Instead of occupying the whole of the site, which planning regulations permitted, we opted for:
a) constructing three separate buildings in order to allow sunlight to pass between them and improve the environmental conditions of the formerly sombre Carrer Roig;
b) rectifying the existing alignment of Carrer Roig, substituting it for another which, funnel-shaped, opens onto Carrer Carme in order to foster the urban—hitherto markedly neighborhood—character of the former;
c) articulating the three buildings between each other and the street by means of covered spaces of different heights and degrees of enclosure;
d) opening the dining rooms on the corners of the buildings so that between the street and the long side of the dwellings visual relationships would be established.

1. Eixample: 19th century Urban extension of Barcelona

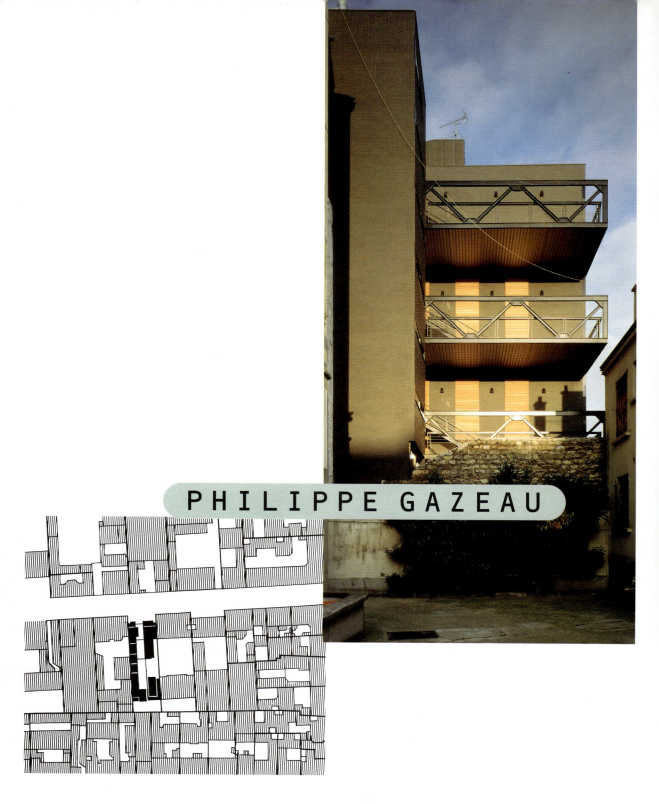

PHILIPPE GAZEAU

Dwellings in the 19th Arrondissement

The heterogeneous urban fabric of the area around the Canal de l'Ourcq, near the Parc de la Villette, was the inspiration for this design, which comprises two linked main buildings surrounding an empty space containing the vertical circulation routes. This gap reveals the great depth of the plot to the passer-by on the road, and allows the activity and light of the street to penetrate into the interior of the block. Happily, this device makes it possible to free the plot from its surroundings and also to develop a distinctive typology linked to the main external staircase. The housing is laid out on this long, narrow plot in four buildings which skillfully accord with the Parisian planning regulations. The design proposes apartments placed crosswise on the site with various orientations, something which seemed not to be possible *a priori* on the existing plot. The site was therefore divided into three parallel bands of unequal lengths which organize the complex on either side of a deep passage that functions as the 'respiratory system' of the block.

▶ Location
PARIS
Architect P. GAZEAU
Collaborators
A. CANTIN, J. FORTE
Design 1991
Construction 1994
Photographs
J.M. MONTHIERS

Apartment facing the interior of the block

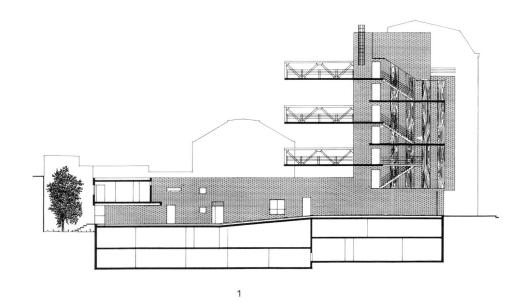

1

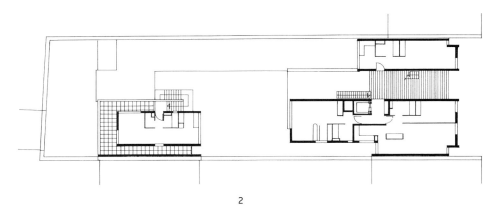

1. Longitudinal section
2. Third floor plan
3. First floor plan
4. Ground floor plan

2

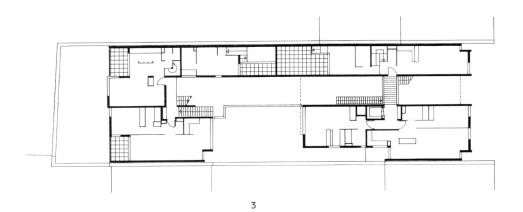

3

4

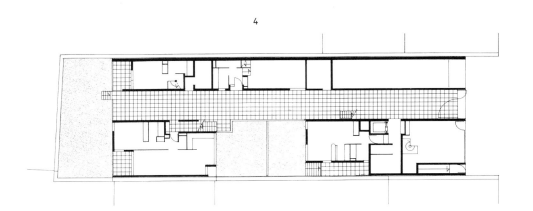

Main exterior staircase

244

FRANCIS SOLER

Housing block

> Location PARÍS
> Architect
> FRANCIS SOLER
> Collaborators
> HABITAT SOCIAL FRANÇAIS
> (Quantity surveyors)
> GEC INGENIERIE (Engineering)
> Project 1991
> Construction 1993
> Photographies
> N. BOREL, O. GELPÍ

Belleville, in Paris, with its very special smells of oriental dishes. We all have in our heads singular images of *The Mysteries of Paris,* of its ruinous corners inhabited by the poorest of the poor. Here, one can still find the dilapidated remains of the end of the 19th century, which are disappearing little by little, swept away by the social hygiene measures implemented for various rehousing schemes.
We are offered a red brick wall. It is a dark, blind gable, against which it is proposed to construct the housing on a site only a few meters deep.
The constraints are such that the project designs itself, as benign as a piece of furniture standing against a wall or a painting hanging in its frame.
The building faces the western sun and the afternoon light is superb. The skin is carefully executed in a burnt earthen tone that reddens in the sunlight of the Passage Saint Caumont. Here, everyone enjoys the right to enter their own home in isolation. These are modern houses, with day rooms on the lower level and bedrooms upstairs, where social conviviality is constantly present.
The neighborliness so talked about these days pays homage more to common sense and to each individual's reality than to the idiotic principle of frenzied alignments with prohibited interruptions.
This means additively creating a city of small fragments.
A way like any other, in effect, of writing urban history.

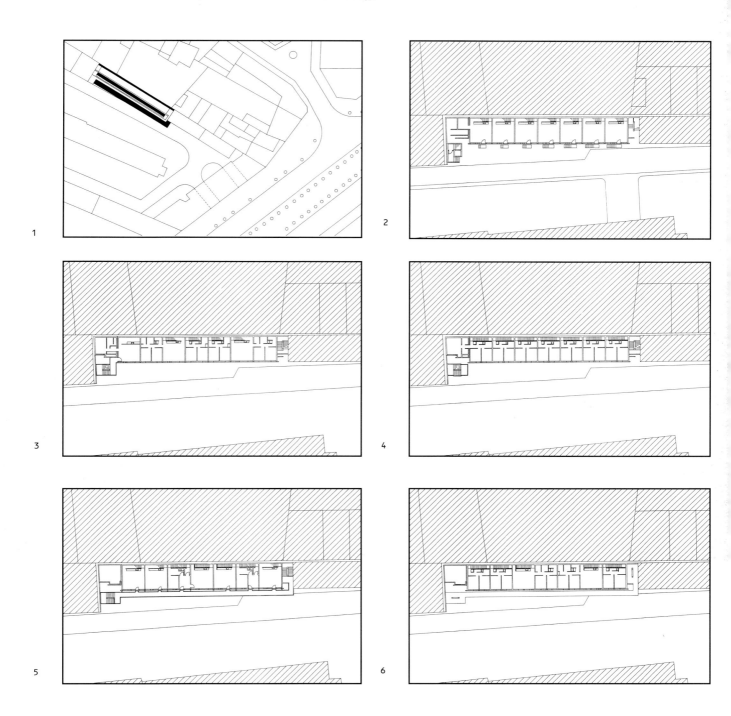

1. Location
2. Ground floor plan
3. First floor plan
4. Second floor plan
5. Third floor plan
6. Fourth floor plan
7. Cross sections

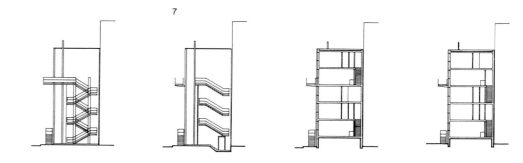

FRANÇOIS MARZELLE
ISABELLE MANESCAU
EDOUARD STEEG

Apartments for immigrants

This new residence is located in the Chartrons district, an area dominated by activities that are on the decline or in the process of changing. The location perhaps presents a certain risk. However, in this case it is one of the advantages of the project: proximity to the city center, easy access to means of transport and shopping centers are important advantages, since they mean that the residents are not isolated, and they make it possible for the most impoverished to maintain themselves within a minimal economic and consumer circuit. The design has an experimental dimension: it envisages living units accommodating five people, each room equipped with individual shower and toilet. The duplex layout of the units made it possible to provide an individual entrance to each room by way of staircases for each two living units located in the patio. The patio space, enlivened by differences in level and by the metal staircases giving access to the rooms, functions as an additional living space. On the lower level, the cafeteria, the laundry and the meeting room open onto this space. Above this, facing each other, are the three-story facades composed of an assembly of openwork wooden shutters fixed to sliding panels. This first skin, protecting a 1.20-meter-wide loggia and the intimacy of the room, allows the tenants to control the entrance of light and the degree of contact they wish to have with the neighbor opposite. The almost blind facade overlooking the street only permits the gaze of the passer-by to filter in through the two full-height splits in the low building. This solution reflects the closed and secret character of the facades characteristic of the district by foiling it, thereby preserving the intimacy of the central space without cutting the interior off from the street.

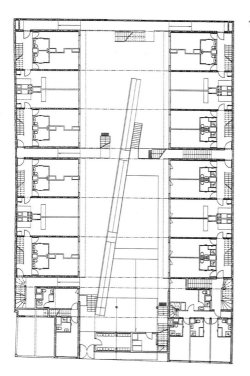

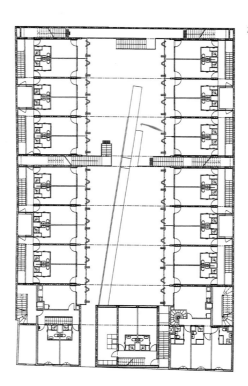

1. Ground floor plan
2. Level 1
3. Level 2
4. Level 3
5. Interior elevation
6. Section

▶ Location
BORDEAUX (FRANCE)
Architect
**FRANÇOIS MARZELLE,
ISABELLE MANESCAU,
EDOUARD STEEG**
Collaborators
J.M. DANCY (Consultor)
Design 1991
Construction 1994
Photographs
V. MONTHIERS, J. SCHOLMOFF

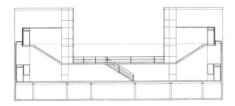

6

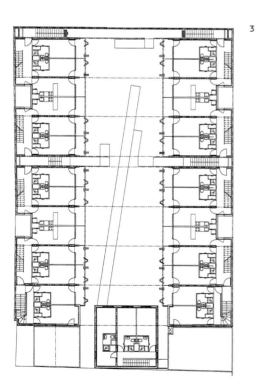

3

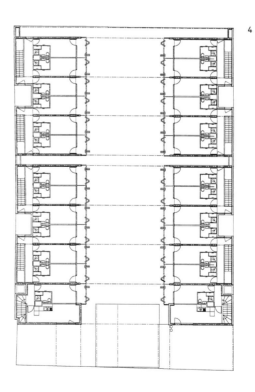

4

5

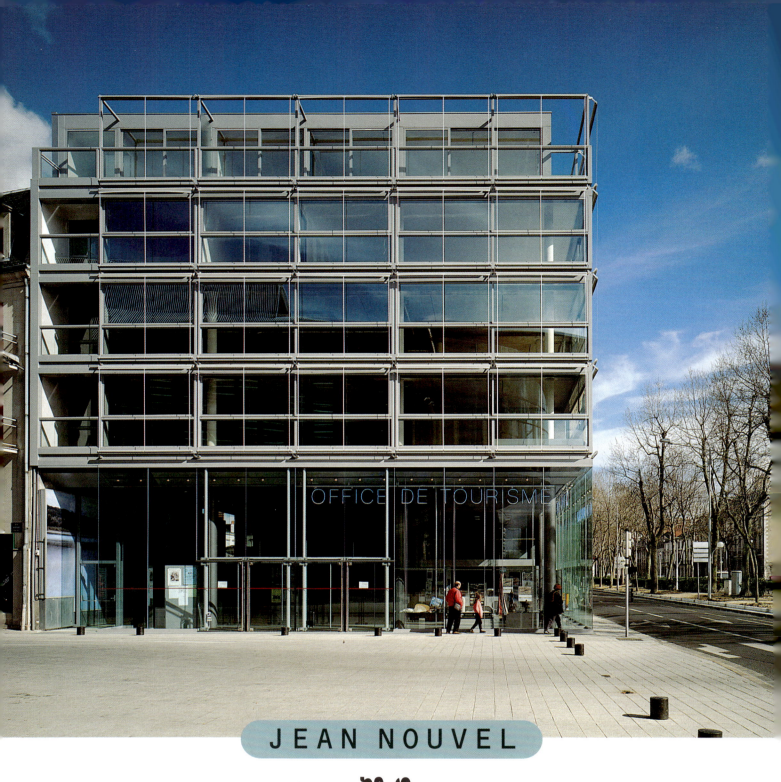

JEAN NOUVEL

Housing and offices

Location TOURS (FRANCE) – Architects JEAN NOUVEL, EMMANUEL CATTANI & ASSOCIÉS – Collaborators DIDIER BRAULT (Project leader) GUILLAUME POTEL (Project coordinator) – Project 1990 – Construction 1993 – Photographs M. DENANCE, J.M.MONTHIERS

An entire quarter was remodelled alongside the construction of the International Congress Center of Tours. The coach station was redesigned, the square situated between the railway station and the congress center was remodelled to cover a new car park with 826 parking spaces, and Rue Bernard-Palissy became a semi-pedestrian thoroughfare. The site is a plot measuring 135 meters long by 55 meters wide, on the corner of Rue Bernard-Palissy and Boulevard Heurteloup. The overall remodelling of this town quarter made it possible to design a coherent urban complex, in which the wealth of 'connections' between the various elements contributes to their integration.
It also provided the ideal means of overcoming a series of functional constrictions, such as access to the International Congress Center for heavy goods vehicles.
With its orthogonal geometry, this building contrasts with the rounded forms of the International Congress Center to create a 'gateway' opening onto the cathedral and old Tours.
This rectilinear, transparent prism housing a mixed program of flats, offices and the main tourist office also provides access for heavy goods vehicles to the International Congress Center via a service tunnel.
The facade picks up the structure of the spaces inside in its adjustable polyester blinds, which vary the entrance of light at the facade.

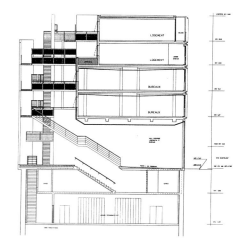

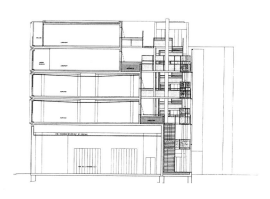

1

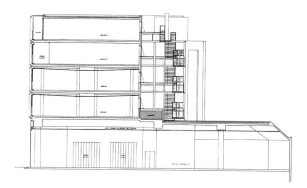

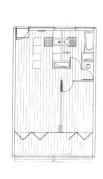
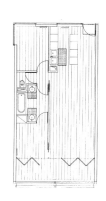
2
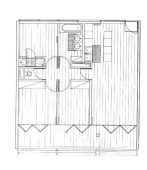
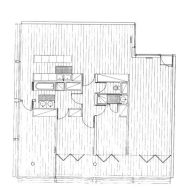

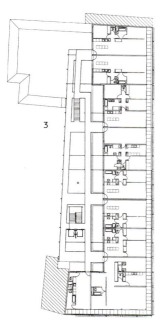 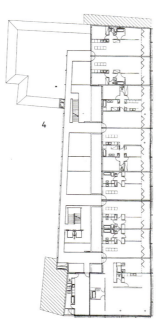 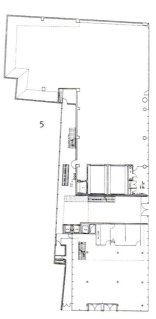

1. Cross sections
2. Dwelling types of two, three, four and five rooms
3. Fourth floor plan
4. Third floor plan
5. Ground floor plan. Tourist office, main hall and goods access to Congress Center

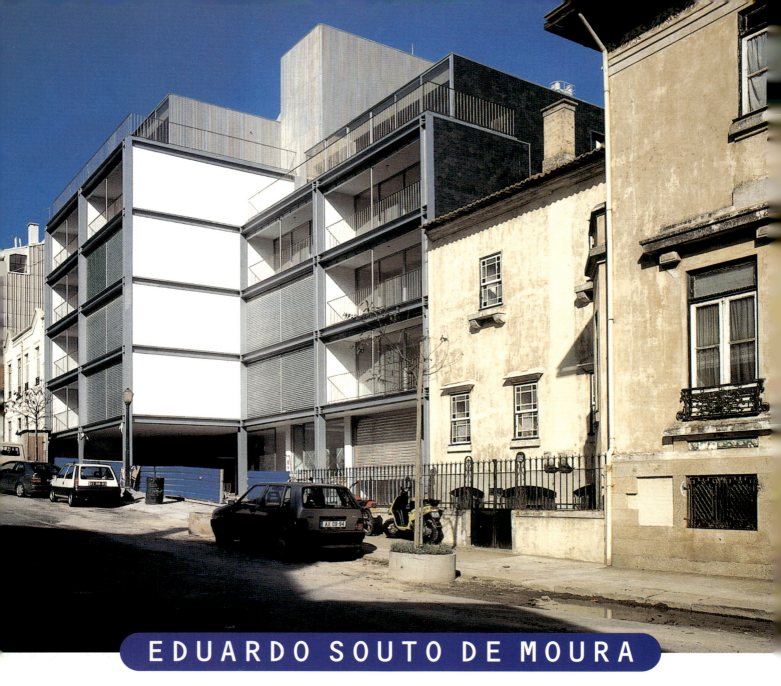

EDUARDO SOUTO DE MOURA

Housing block

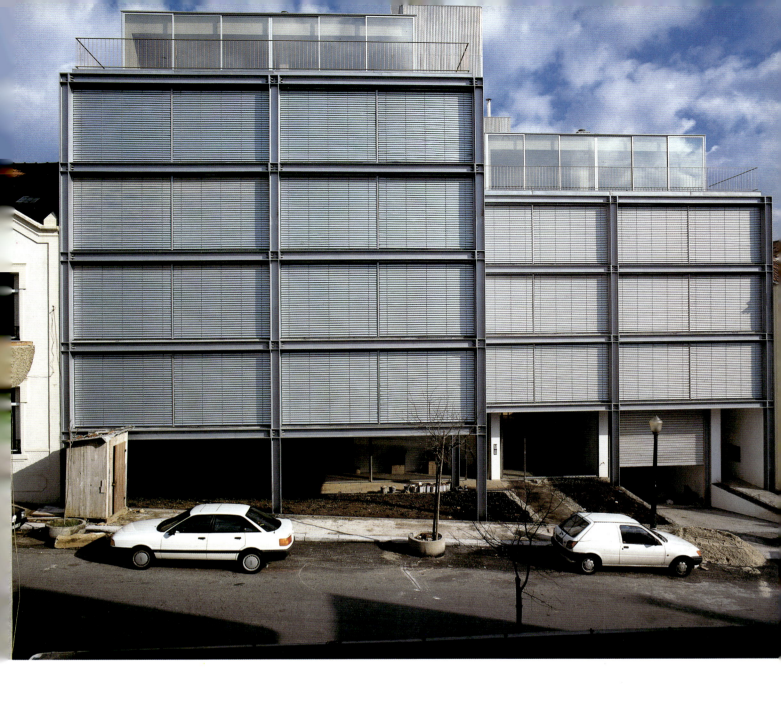

When in the 18th century Oporto expanded beyond its medieval walls, the properties on the periphery were subdivided and developed in long, narrow plots in order to adapt to the topography of the land.
The houses, long and narrow in turn, were built from prefabricated elements of dressed stone, so that the openings were defined almost *a priori*. The other parts were generally faced with brick on the main facade, with zinc sheeting on the secondary facades and pieces of slate on the sides. This building follows the same tradition, not through mimicry but in terms of construction principles.
The stone structure has been replaced by iron rebars, while the same facings of zinc and slate have been preserved. There is no direct correspondence between the simplicity of a criterion and its reification. Transformations in architecture are neither as rapid nor as evident as they seem in compendiums and manuals. It is necessary to progress through the project and construction stages in order to reach banality.

▶ Location OPORTO
Architect
EDUARDO SOUTO DE MOURA
Collaborators
GRAÇA CORREIA,
PEDRO MENDES,
SILVIA ALVES,
FRANCISCO CUNHA,
MANUELA LARA (Project)
CODIO (Structural engineering)
Contractors
SOARES DA COSTA/SAN JOSÉ
Project 1992
Construction 1995
Photographs
LUÍS FERREIRA ALVES

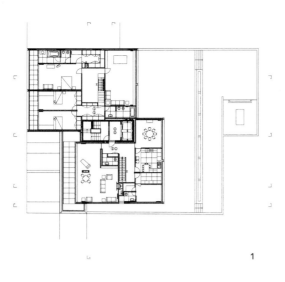

1

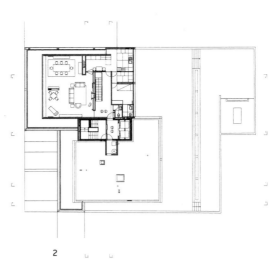

2

3

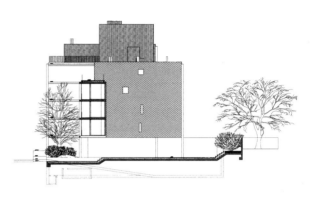

4

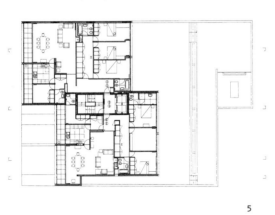

5

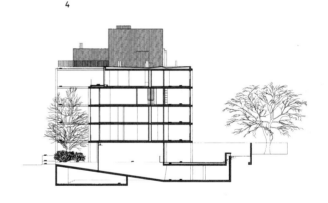

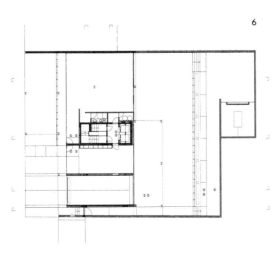

6

1. Fourth floor plan
   Access to duplex type A
   and duplex type B
2. Fifth floor plan
   Access to duplex type B
3. Third floor plan
   Typical floor of dwelling
   and duplex type A
4. Sections
5. First and second floor plans
   Typical floor of dwelling
6. Ground floor
   Access to dwellings and parking

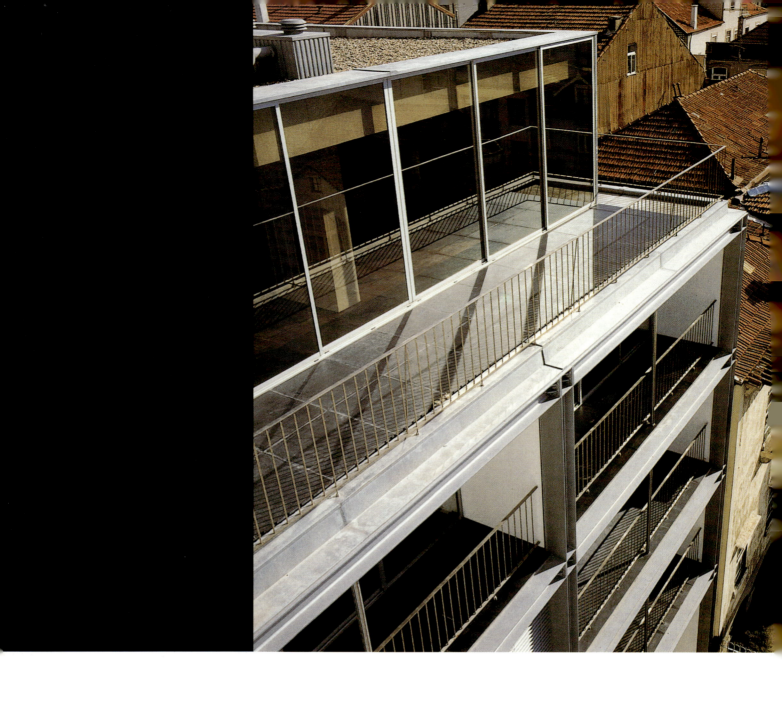

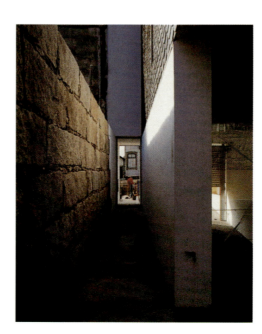
View of access to inner court

KEIM & SILL

Prefabricated housing and work units

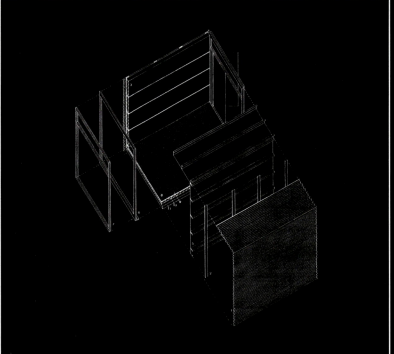

The project involves the
of an old building located
of Rathenow, near Berlin,
has been reconditioned a
rear (garden patio) facad
twelve assembled and fit
containers have been hou
means of a structure of c
beams, the aim being to
the building's width by 4
The exterior facade has u
no alteration.
An engineering studio is
on the ground and first f
All possible walls have be
eliminated, leaving two a
open work spaces which
accommodate 20 employ
The container area has b
over to the partitioned-o
and spaces needed in an
conference rooms, toilets
kitchens, an office, a roo
photocopier and other fa
Three apartments of betv
and 90 m² have been buil
these, by following the sa
principle and integrating
containers in the housing
For economic and technic
the containers have been
constructed some 500 k
their final emplacement.
Due to their size, road tr
possible, as is their hand
by crane. Fabrication and
has been realized with re
construction industry ma
the concrete structure o
they rest is also designe
security measure in case

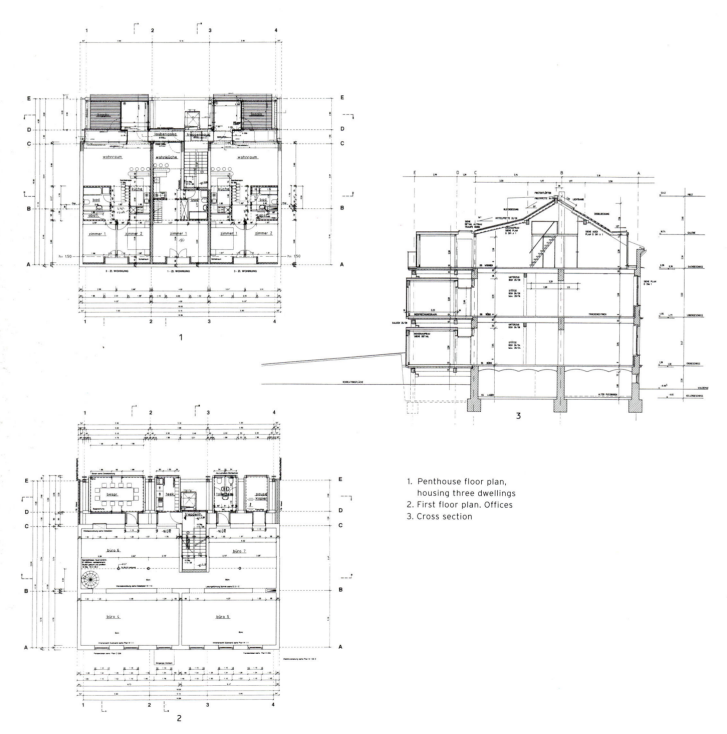

1. Penthouse floor plan, housing three dwellings
2. First floor plan. Offices
3. Cross section

Location RATHENOW (GERMANY) – Architects JOCHEN KEIM, KLAUS SILL – Collaborators HANNES MOSER, MARTIN MARSCHNER. ROHWER (Structural engineer) – Contractor ELFRIEDE DAU, FLENSBURG – Project 1995 Construction 1997 – Photographs GRUPO 96, J. PIZARRO & CH. GEBLER

HOUSING
NEW ALTERNATIVES, NEW SYSTEMS

Housing: new alternatives - new systems

Author Manuel Gausa

Collaborator Jaime Salazar

Assistance Brigitte Hübner

Graphic design Ramon Prat, Rosa Lladó

Production Font i Prat Ass. SL, Barcelona

Translation Paul Hammond

Printing Ingoprint S.A.
D. L. B-6959/98

A CIP catalogue record for this book is available
from the Library of Congress, Washington D.C., USA

Deutsche Bibliothek Cataloging-in-Publication Data
Housing : new alternatives - new systems /
Manuel Gausa. [Translation from Spanish into Engl.:
Paul Hammond]

Basel ; Boston ; Berlin : Birkhäuser ;
Barcelona : Actar, 1998
ISBN 3-7643-5870-X (Basel...)
ISBN 0-8176-5870-X (Boston)

This work is subject to copyright. All rights are
reserved, whether the whole or part of the material
is concerned, specifically the rights of translation,
reprinting, re-use of illustrations, recitation,
broadcasting, reproduction on microfilms or in
other ways, and storage in data banks.
For any kind of use, permission of the copyright
owner must be obtained.

© 1998 Actar Publishers, Barcelona, Spain
Roca i Batlle 2-4, 08023 Barcelona
Tel 34.3 418 49 93 Fax 34.3 412 39 64
arquitec@actar.es www.actar.es
Birkhäuser – Verlag für Architektur, P.O.Box 133,
CH-4010 Basel, Switzerland
Printed on acid-free paper produced from
chlorine-free pulp. TCF ∞
Printed in Spain
ISBN 3-7643-5870-X
ISBN 0-8176-5870-X

9 8 7 6 5 4 3 2 1